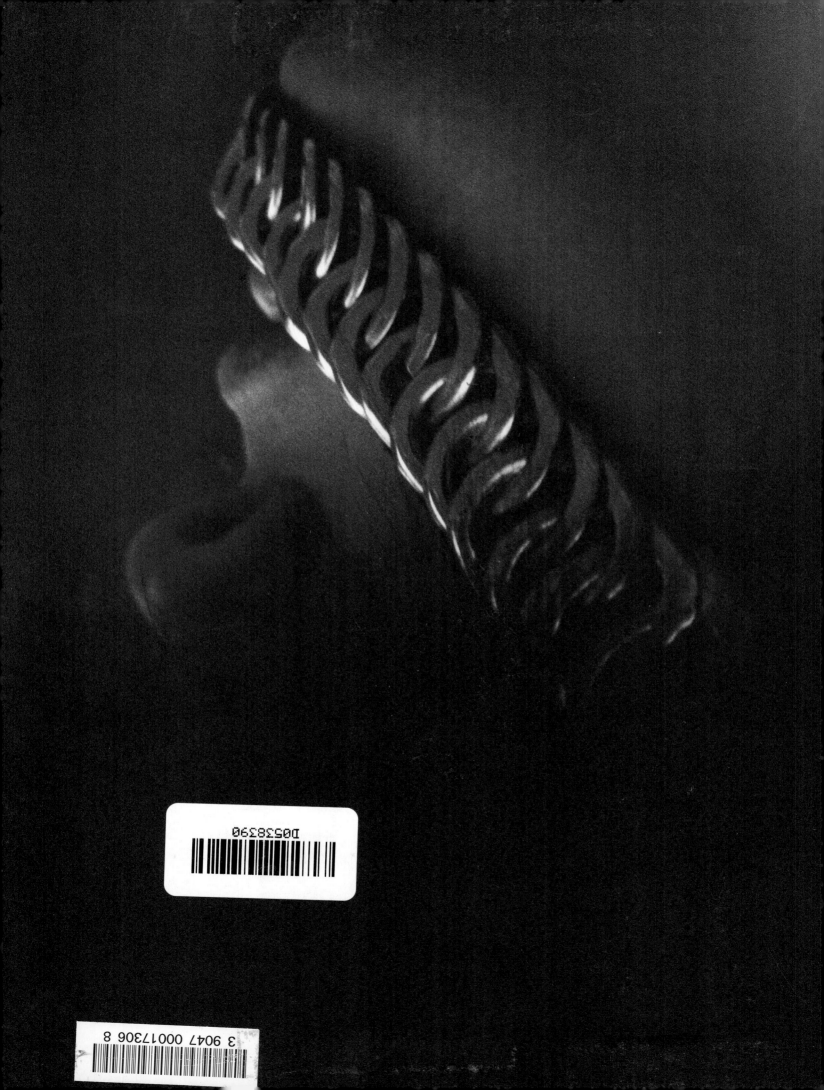

THE GUARDS

THE GUARDS

Photographed by
Anthony Edgeworth

Written by
John de St. Jorre

Designed by
Samuel N. Antupit

Ridge Press/Crown Publishers Inc. New York

The photographs in this book were taken with Nikon cameras and Nikkor lenses in formats ranging from 20mm to 1000mm. Mr. Edgeworth used Kodak films exclusively in producing these photographs.

Library of Congress Cataloging in Publication Data
Edgeworth, Anthony.
  The Guards.
  1. Great Britain. Army. Household Division.
I. De St. Jorre, John. II. Title.
UA649.5.E33   355.3'1'0941   80-26781
ISBN 0-517-54376-1
Printed in Japan by Dai Nippon   10 9 8 7 6 5 4 3 2 1
First Edition

Contents

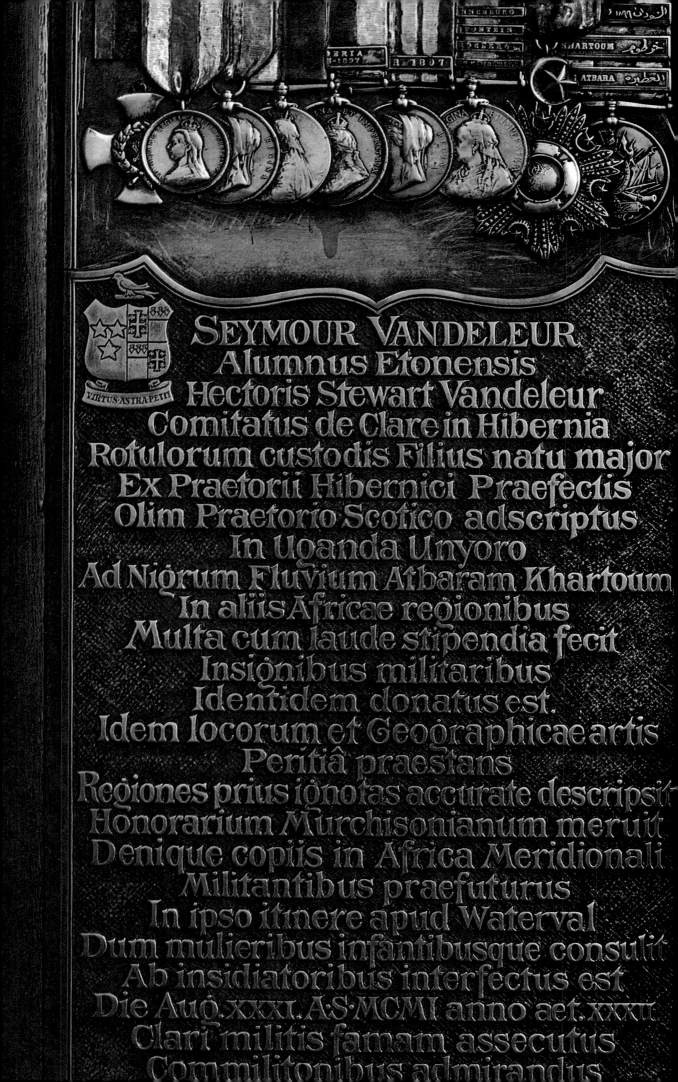

SEYMOUR VANDELEUR
Alumnus Etonensis
Hectoris Stewart Vandeleur
Comitatus de Clare in Hibernia
Rotulorum custodis Filius natu major
Ex Praetorii Hibernici Praefectis
Olim Praetorio Scotico adscriptus
In Uganda Unyoro
Ad Nigrum Fluvium Atbaram Khartoum
In aliis Africae regionibus
Multa cum laude stipendia fecit
Insignibus militaribus
Identidem donatus est.
Idem locorum et Geographicae artis
Peritiâ praestans
Regiones prius ignotas accurate descripsit
Honorarium Murchisonianum meruit
Denique copiis in Africa Meridionali
Militantibus praefuturus
In ipso itinere apud Waterval
Dum mulieribus infantibusque consulit
Ab insidiatoribus interfectus est
Die Aug. XXXI. A.S. MCMI anno aet. XXXII
Clari militis famam assecutus
Commilitonibus admirandus

VIRTUS ASTRA PETIT

Foreword

To James Boswell, a respecter of tradition, they were the "brilliant" guards whose special task of protecting the sovereign has had more than symbolic meaning in the uneven evolution of the British monarchy. The London populace saw them rather differently, as heavy-booted keepers of the king's peace, whose popularity rose in direct proportion to their distance from the capital. For the foreign tourist they remain a source of endless fascination but to London taxi drivers, faithful to the dissenting view, they are a pain in the neck.

The Guards, most easily recognized in their toy soldier uniforms marching up and down outside the royal palaces in London and Windsor, are a unique and deceptive military institution. They are simultaneously dedicated practitioners of the military parade, to which they bring the expertise and flair of a Broadway musical, and a superbly disciplined force of fighting men exchanging their scarlet tunics for a flak jacket or a parachute smock with the easy rhythm of their marching step.

That duality is interesting but perhaps not too interesting. What makes the Guards, a body of some fifty-five hundred officers and men grouped under the homely title of Household Division, worthy of closer inspection is the way in which such a history-encrusted relic has survived, displaying outward vigor and inward confidence, well into the closing stages of the twentieth century.

They are a microcosm of the British army's regimental structure with its emphasis on local geography and family ties. They are also a self-regenerating elite, a jealous tribal entity, an unofficial employment agency, a subtle but influential component of the British establishment, and a cameo preserved in military aspic of attitudes and manners largely left behind by the modern world.

They are, in the words of one of their officers, a two-faced Janus, looking forward as modern infantrymen and armored cavalry to the Third World War and coping with an increasingly sophisticated

Plaque in Eton College chapel honoring a Guards officer (opposite page)

and relentless enemy in Northern Ireland. And yet they seem to be equally absorbed by the miracle of their continuing separateness, their enduring sense of family, their almost feminine obsession with clothes, their unquestioning devotion to the sovereign whose own survival so intimately governs their own, their submission to the tyranny of the ceremonial, and their fondness for the quirks and nonsense of military titles, customs and traditions that have been faithfully handed down through the long centuries.

The public view of the Guards has a Janus-like quality too. One segment of British society sees them as a set of privileged, wealthy, ineffective "poofters," harmless enough but only justified by the amount of hard cash they bring in from the tourist trade. The other group regards them as a glittering symbol of all that is good about the British way of life, an example of the nation's genius for retaining something that may be a trifle old-fashioned but is still self-evidently excellent, like a Rolls Royce or a Saville Row suit.

Both views are, we think, flawed. The first is shallow and obsolete; the second smug and insular. The truth lies, as if often does, somewhere in between. There are, however, criticisms that can be levelled at the Guards which they themselves do not refute. They are elitist, racist and sexist. Yet while admitting the charges and aware that other famous military formations, like the United States Marine Corps and the Israeli army, have successfully opened their doors to all classes, races and even to women, they will painstakingly explain why it has to be so. A large influx of middle or working class officers? A black or brown face under a bearskin? A *woman* in the scarlet tunic? (The Queen, of course, is another matter.) Unthinkable.

Yet one of the striking things about the Guards is that they have, in common with the rest of the British establishment, learnt the difficult Darwinian lesson of evolution, adapting to survive. Their European rivals, the Russian Guards, the famous Prussian regiments, Napoleon's Imperial Guard and so on, have all faded into history. Unlike the Bourbons who learnt nothing and forgot nothing the Guards remember everything and have absorbed quite a lot too. They know the limits of their power and influence, they have the ability to laugh at their eccentricities and they recognize the wind of change when they feel it on their cheek. As a result, Her Majesty's five regiments of Foot Guards and two regiments of Household Cavalry can be seen in one uniform or another wherever the British army is called upon to soldier—in the jungles of Central America, the mean streets of Belfast, the heaths of northern Germany, the mountains of Cyprus or marching to the beat of the drum along the Mall in the heart of London.

What is the secret of the Guards' appeal? They are undeniably elegant, stylish, colorful and highly professional. The sculpted lines of scarlet and black of the Grenadiers on the march, the sunlight dancing off the Life Guards' cuirasses, the skirl of the pipes of the Scots and Irish and the rich texture of the brass of the massed Guards' bands during one of London's great military parades will send a frisson of pleasure down the most unmilitary of backs. By simply being there the Guards evoke the glory and pathos of the past in the way that a painting or a piece of architecture sometimes does. Their daily presence is a reminder of the great commanders and great battles of history, of Marlborough and Blenheim, of Wellington and Waterloo, of the retreat to Corunna, the bloody melees in the Crimea, the slaughterhouse on the Somme and the dark days of Dunkirk.

Some people, especially foreigners, enjoy the stereotype. The Guards' mannerisms, often deliberately exaggerated with tongue in cheek to sustain the image, are expected to conform to the lifestyle of Edwardian England. Many are fascinated by what might be called the peacock syndrome, the phenomenon associated with soldiers who spend much of their waking day preparing their uniform and climbing in and out of it. And not a few, one suspects, admire the arrogance that has traditionally been a part of the make-up of elite military units since the time of the Romans, though once again the reality behind the plumage is somewhat different.

Our aim has been to investigate this company of men which has had a continuous corporate body and soul since the middle of the seventeenth century, to look at the wet civilian clay as it is poured into the military mold and to see how the different layers that make the whole are constructed. The young recruit is "kicked to excellence," as one officer expressed it, not literally these days but through a long and arduous period of training. The non-commissioned officers, as in most armies, are a tough, hard-drinking crowd—shrewd, sly, generous— but good people to know when the bullets are whistling overhead. They keep the system going and the pecking order rigid in the best traditions of the English butler whose power rests on his control over the kitchen and his indispensability to the drawing-room.

The officer corps remains a select though no longer a monied affair. Once inside, however, it is a different matter. Everyone in the Guards seems to know everyone else. Outside, their tentacles spread through the landed gentry, the business world, diplomacy, politics, the church and even the theatre. Their ranks, past and present, are a litany of famous Britons. For better or worse, they remain a military aristocracy without parallel in the Western world.

Our book is not an "official" or "authorized" account. The Household Division agreed to help us and we agreed to submit the text and pictures to a test of factual accuracy. It is neither a hagiography nor an exposé. We have merely stretched the canvas and allowed the men of the Guards to step forward through the medium of the camera and the tape recorder. We have touched up and framed the result. The book lays no claim to being an historical study for that was not our purpose. Most Guardsmen either do not know or care to talk about their history; but it seems to tick away in their subconscious and is a tangible ingredient in their collective personality. We hope, through osmosis, we have acquired a little of that historical sense and that it informs our work.

The book is, without apology, a piece of journalism designed to examine and record. Who are the Guards and why are they still around? Those are the questions we have posed ourselves and in trying to answer them we have travelled and worked as a team with the result that the normal distinctions between photographer, writer and designer became blurred. We believe that something positive emerged from that fusion of roles and modest talents and that it is reflected in the final product. We hope also that Oliver Cromwell, in whose Model Army the first of the Guards regiments was formed, would approve when we declare our aim to be a representative portrait, "warts and all."

Acknowledgments

We would like to pay tribute to the two most recent books on "Guardology," Russell Braddon's *All the Queen's Men* and Julian Paget's *The Story of the Guards*. Both, in their different ways, are excellent accounts and we learnt much from them, a learning that is particularly reflected in the historical appendices to this book.

We are specially indebted to Major R.A.G. Courage and his small and helpful staff in the public relations office at Horse Guards. They not only efficiently directed our travels to the far-flung units of the Household Division—from Belize in Central America to Berlin in East Germany—but placed their own valuable stock of expertise and Guards' lore at our disposal.

We would also like to thank Major General Sir John Swinton for granting us permission to do the book and his successor, Major General Desmond Langley, for endorsing that decision and sharing some of his thoughts with us. We hasten to add that the opinions reached here are our own and that no one should be blamed for them—or for any errors—but ourselves.

Throughout we adopted a policy of anonymity for those we interviewed and feel it best to adhere to the same principle here. We would, however, like to express our deep gratitude to all the members of the Household Division—in Pirbright, Sandhurst, Windsor, London, Belize, South Armagh, Detmold, and Berlin—who gave up their valuable time to pose for us, talk to us and show us what they do and how they live.

The Guards have been called many things, good and bad, but snobbery is not in their lexicon whereas hospitality—sometimes lavish to the point of sinking us and the project—is written on every page. Guardsmen of all ranks were unfailingly kind, co-operative and frank and we are deeply appreciative.

A number of people who once served in the Guards but have now gone on to distinguish themselves in a great variety of ways also helped us. We would like to thank Major General Sir Allan Adair, the Archbishop of Canterbury, Lord Carrington, Viscount De L'Isle, the Earl of Lichfield, and Colonel David Stirling. Our thanks are due to the Provost of Eton and we owe much to Mr. Bartle Bull, Mr. Matthew Bull, Mrs. Sarah d'Erlanger, Lord Grenfell, Mr. Timothy Tufnell, and Lt. Colonel David Webb-Carter all of whom gave us excellent advice and moral support when we most needed it.

Anthony Edgeworth,
John de St. Jorre,
Samuel N. Antupit.

New York, September 1980

Part I

From Cradle to Grave

Crossmaglen, Northern Ireland

Market Square in Crossmaglen looks, at first glance, like a thousand other small country towns. There is a red telephone booth, a small post office, the Glen Cafe, Mr. Cusker's Barber's Shop, McEntee's Family Butcher, and Keenan's Pub. Framing the square are solid rows of two-story houses, some with brightly painted doors. Small cars move around, a dog lifts its leg on a lamppost, and women in head scarves stop and chat with each other as they go about their shopping.

But in what ordinary market town would you be watching this scene from a television monitor screen in a fortress with a mortarproof ceiling, protected by a company of Guardsmen tense and ready for battle.

A patrol of four Welsh Guardsmen, wearing flak jackets and carrying their rifles in the crooks of their arms, walk warily out into the square. A few paces behind them crawls a Saracen armored troop carrier, eight tons of reinforced steel, with the machine-gunner's helmeted head sticking out of the hatch.

It is a day of soft Irish rain. Yesterday was a day of medium Irish rain and tomorrow could well be a day of heavy Irish rain. The Guardsmen patrolling the town will get wet, and their elusive Irish Republican Army enemy, content to bide its time, will stay dry.

Crossmaglen is a tight-mouthed, narrow-eyed village of some two thousand people, sitting uncomfortably on the Ulster-Irish border. It is Catholic and Republican to a man. Within ninety seconds of shooting a British soldier or detonating a bomb, a gunman can be in the Irish Republic, safe from pursuit. When a British soldier lies dying on the street, the townsfolk avert their eyes and pass by. It is, despite appearances, a place of ancient hatred and present fear.

The Welsh Guardsmen, barely out of their teens, circle cautiously around the square. Their fingers are on their triggerguards, their eyes search for the movement that could mean a high-velocity bullet in the belly or the brain. For four and a half months, with only one four-day break, they will patrol the town and surrounding countryside for up to eighteen hours a day. They will be constantly wet, often tired, and rarely out of danger. The statistical odds are that during their tour of duty two of them will die or be seriously injured. Yet, so skilled and elusive is their enemy, they will probably never have the fighting soldier's satisfaction of striking back.

A statue has been erected in Market Square, one hundred yards from the barricaded police station that serves as the army's base. It is an emaciated figure in bronze, the face uplifted in a rictus of agony. It represents the yearning spirit of Irish freedom and, by implication, the continuing yoke of British oppression. The inscription, in Gaelic and English, reads:

GLORY TO YOU ALL, PRAISED AND HUMBLE HEROES
WHO HAVE WILLINGLY SUFFERED FOR YOUR UNSELFISH
AND PASSIONATE LOVE OF IRISH FREEDOM.

Crossmaglen is an integral part of the United Kingdom of Great Britain and Northern Ireland and, in theory, as British as Berkshire. To keep it that way, and to protect the police, the soldiers are needed. To serve a summons for the simplest misdemeanor, say a parking offense, a policeman has to be escorted by four Welsh Guardsmen. But simply by being there, the army presents a much more tempting target to the IRA gunmen who live across the border. No one has yet been able to find a way of breaking this vicious circle.

Crossmaglen police station is surrounded by 24-foot-high walls. Two *sangars*—raised observation and gun platforms—give it a fortresslike appearance. Television cameras with zoom lenses and windshield wipers overlook Cullaville Street and Market Square. There is an 80-foot television antenna above the building, and the Union Jack and the red-dragon standard of the Welsh Guards fly overhead. A Beau Geste fort in an Irish bog.

The solders live in cramped quarters in the police station. There are eighteen to a room stacked in three-tiered bunks, accommodations as claustrophobic as those in a submarine. For the soldiers there is only one way out of Crossmaglen, and that is by helicopter. The narrow, winding country roads are too dangerous. Daily helicopter flights bring in food, milk, mail, the padre, and the paymaster. And out, by the same means, go the sick, the wounded, the dead, and the rubbish.

The police station is having a face-lift. New mortarproof walls and roofs are being built by army engineers. Every three months a whole battalion of infantry is deployed to clear the road to Crossmaglen so that a single resupply convoy may enter, the sort of operation that used to be commonplace in the remote and far more exotic corners of the British Empire. Now "bandit country" is next door, in South Armagh.

Since 1972 the British army has lost fifty soldiers in this area. One hundred more have been wounded, half of them seriously. In the same period the IRA has lost half a dozen men. The countryside, dotted with small farms and peacefully grazing cattle, is no friendlier than the town. Shortly after the Welsh Guards arrived, a patrol crossed a country road and a remote-controlled bomb went off. Two men were safely over and the last was still on the other side. The third Guardsman, in the middle of the road at the time of the explosion, disappeared. One of his friends called out, "Come off it, mate, where are you hiding?" There was a huge hole in the road but no sign of a corpse. Pieces of the young soldier were still being found the next day. They were collected, put into a plastic bag, and taken out with the mail by helicopter.

"At the end of our tour," said an officer, "there is a sense of achievement. We don't know quite what we have achieved, but we feel we have done something."

Both the violence in Northern Ireland—Britain's only and seemingly endless war—and the Guards who are dispatched to deal with it have ancient roots. Both also share a sense of continuity. A Welsh Guards sergeant at Crossmaglen was talking about a notorious IRA gunman. "We'll get him," he said. "Or if we don't," he added as an afterthought, "my son will when he joins the Welsh Guards."

Joining the Guards: Twenty-five Years Ago

"The British forces have nothing but generals,
admirals and bands."
—General George S. Brown,
former Chairman of the U.S. Joint Chiefs of Staff.

An old soldier describing how it used to be: "I was living in London and a friend, also from Ireland, persuaded me to go along to the local recruiting office. We both wanted to join the REME [Royal Electrical and Mechanical Engineers]. Well, anyway, this fella came in. He was about six foot five in his stockinged feet, so that made him about six foot nine in his boots. 'What are you doing here?' he said. I spoke up and said I was joining the army. 'Where are you from?' 'Dublin,' I said. 'You're joining the Irish Guards,' he said. 'No, I'm bloody not,' I said, 'I'm joining the REME.' He got me by the scruff of the neck and dragged me into another room. 'Look, lad,' he said, 'you want to be with your own kind. The Irish Guards.' I'd never heard of the bloody Irish Guards. He produced a lot of photographs of men in big hats and red tunics and all. He was wearing immaculate blues, Number One dress, with a big badge of rank and a forage cap with a slashed peak, and I thought he looked great. 'This is the kit you wear,' he said. Well, that was that. I joined the Guards."

Today

An army recruiting office in west London. This area is a traditional recruiting zone for the Queens Regiment (a line infantry regiment) and the Royal Irish Hussars (a line cavalry regiment). Other regiments are not allowed to poach if a recruit asks for either of those units. But they can advertise in the window, and there is a display of the wide variety of head gear worn by different regiments. The slogan above it reads: GET A HAT GET AHEAD. In the center sits a bearskin.

Inside the office there is a tall Grenadier Guards Color Sergeant. "When a young lad comes in," he says, "we'll take down his name, date of birth, and all that and check his record. Any crime—

New recruits' first day at the Guards depot, eyeing a "veteran" (pages 24–25)
Uniform issue after the medical examination (pages 26–27)
Recruits, army suitcases in hand, being escorted by a Coldstream Guards NCO to their billets (pages 28–29)

we've got a cop shop just over the road—and we stop right there. Mind you, if he took a couple of wheels off a pram to make a go-cart, we'll ignore that. Then he does some tests and comes back for an interview with the recruiting officer. After his medical and references have been checked we write him up and recommend him—or not. I've sold the army to him; now he's got to sell himself to me. What do we look for in a future Guardsman? Well, we accept anyone if he is over five foot eight inches, has a clean record, is of good appearance—assuming he's white of course." He laughs. "Everybody takes blacks except us.

"The yardstick is, would you have that man in your platoon? If you wouldn't, don't put him in some other poor man's unit. We look for high quality. If he has a family connection then he goes straight into that regiment. The soldiers are looked after better in the Guards than any of the other regiments. They are looked after all their lives through our old comrade associations and regimental headquarters." Does Ireland put people off? "Well, our Asian friends won't go there, but apart from that it doesn't make much difference. It's no more dangerous over there than crossing a road."

Pirbright, Surrey. The Guards Depot

It is a golden Indian summer day, a day scores of young men will never forget—the day they took the "Queen's shilling" and joined the army. All afternoon busloads of new recruits are dumped at the depot. As they line up to be registered they look dazed but not frightened; their hair is long, their clothes garish, their luggage various. Total uniformity, the army's first and perhaps most chilling lesson, is imminent as they are issued their new equipment, which includes their uniform and a stunningly unimaginative army suitcase.

The Guards machine is all around them, grinding its gears a little as it absorbs the raw material. Recruits who have been in for a week or so—the process, like digestion and excretion, is continuous—are marching by in squads on the main square, "God's Acre," as the non-commissioned officers (NCO's) call it. Young, red-faced automatons, they move jerkily, their arms swinging high and their rear ends twitching. The drill sergeants snap at their heels like irritable terriers.

Groups of real soldiers pass by, their pace calmer and more rhythmic, on their way to the rifle range or the assault course. In the distance there is the rattle of gunfire and, carried by the breeze, the skirl of bagpipes. The breeze also brings those perennial army smells: creosote, stale food, and sweat.

At any one time there are between eight hundred and a thousand recruits in training at Pirbright. The depot not only turns out trained soldiers for the Household Division but also instructs the rest of the British army's NCO's and a large contingent of foreigners in the art of ceremonial drill. Why the emphasis on drill? "It produces pride in self and teamwork," says a strapping Welsh Guards Regimental sergeant major. "The Guards' record proves the value of the relationship between the square and the battlefield. Bad drill means bad discipline, which means a poor fighting record."

On God's Acre a drill sergeant is warming up a squad that will be passing out shortly. "Quick *march*! Yak, yak, yak, yak . . . About *turn*, right *turn*, left *turn*, change *step*, left *turn* . . . Yak, yak, yak, yak . . . Squad HALT! Are we sufficiently warmed up? Are we?" Red faces nod assent along the ranks. "Good. Quick MARCH! Yak, yak, yak, yak . . . About *turn*, right *turn*, left *turn* . . . Yak, yak, yak, yak. . . ."

Although the ritual of the induction has not changed much over the years—registration, medical, quartermaster's store, soft-shoulder chat with the padre, pep talk from the Company Commander—the tone has. The army is much gentler with its aspiring soldiers than it used to be. There is, initially, very little military emphasis. Instead the lads play games, start breaking in their kit, and get to know their way around the depot.

There are a number of reasons for that. The young men are more impressionable, better educated, and less mature than they were in the days when they left school at fourteen and kicked around for two years before they came into the army. Their parents are less likely to have been in the army, since compulsory military service ended in the early sixties. The result is that, in order to hang on to good potential soldiers, the army has to make the difficult transition from civilian to miliary life more palatable.

Of course, it doesn't always work. A number will fall by the wayside anyway. Some will go AWOL (absent without leave) because of incontrovertible incompatibility, overwhelming homesickness, or an intricate personal relationship that cannot be so brutally interrupted, like the young recruit who couldn't tarry any longer because he had to see his goldfish.

But the time-tested basics of military training remain. The young man who comes in at seventeen or eighteen can expect a tough five-month stint, during which he will reach a peak of physical fitness and disciplined reaction that he probably never thought himself capable of. The Guards' basic training is probably tougher than any in the British army, with the exception of the Parachute Regiment. And no one leaves until he has reached the requisite standard.

"If a recruit can't get it right he can't leave the depot," says a member of the staff. "And if he can't leave the depot he can't become a Guardsman."

Since ceremonial is so much a part of the life of a Guardsman, "bull" (or "spit 'n' polish") takes up a great deal of his time. His kit has to be broken in: boots burnt, beeswaxed, and bulled; bayonet scabbard scraped and painted black; belts and scabbard holder "blancoed" (whitened). A recruit can spend up to three hours a night cleaning, polishing, and burnishing.

But these days he will be sitting in a warm and reasonably comfortable barrack room with angled alcoves, more bed and locker space than ever before, and an enormous and well-cooked meal in his belly. (The choice, quantity, and quality of the food at Pirbright is one of the wonders of the new military age.) Television and films will be available for his entertainment, if he has the time and energy left to watch, and his pay, though not lavish, will accumulate satisfactorily while he has little inclination and less opportunity to spend it during those busy five months.

In the evenings, while he is converting spit and Kiwi polish into a matchless mirror on the toe of his boots, he will learn why the Grenadiers are the senior though not the oldest regiment of Foot Guards, how the Coldstream and Scots held Hougoumont at Waterloo and so turned the French tide, who gives sprigs of shamrock to the Irish Guards each St. Patrick's Day, and why the Welsh Guards were formed in the middle of the First World War.

The Brigade Squad

Among the many groups of young men marching to and fro at Pirbright, one squad looks a little different. The difference is not great, but it is there: a slightly keener look, an air of purpose, something in the facial bones—a patrician sensibility, perhaps. In the mess hall they tend to sit apart from the rest of the recruits, but it is only when you get within earshot that you know for certain that these young men really are very different indeed. Their voices, accents, mannerisms, and above all their self-confidence, reveal them to be "officer material," people who, providing they make the grade, will one day command the men now sharing the miseries of basic training.

Potential officers are sent to join the Brigade Squad by the regimental headquarters of the seven regiments that make up the Household Division. At those headquarters in London they have been interviewed and assessed; their school records have been checked; friends and relatives have been questioned and the ubiquitous and intricately woven Guards grapevine consulted. Pirbright accepts them automatically on regimental headquarters' advice: no questions asked.

These young men still come principally from Britain's public (i.e., private) schools. "Eton and the Guards" has become a cliché, but that ancient school continues to be the largest single contributor, providing five members out of seventeen in one Brigade Squad we met and eight out of thirty-one in another.

Eton College

The courtyard is awash with autumn light as Etonians, large and small, saunter across the quadrangle in their white ties and tails. A weather-worn statue of King Henry VI, the school's fifteenth-century founder, gazes down benignly at an institution as deeply rooted in the soil of England as the monarchy itself. Eton, with thirteen hundred boys in residence, provides a large segment of the officer corps of the British army. This is not surprising, because it is the only school in Britain that, since 1860, has had a full-time career army officer permanently attached to it to train the college's cadet corps. The officer assigned to the job is either a Guardsman or a Green Jacket (the army's elite light infantry regiment). As might be expected, a large number of Etonians choose the Guards or the Royal Green Jackets for a career.

Eton, like many other public schools, produces the qualities in its boys that the army most cherishes: confidence, maturity, leadership, and the ability to talk to—and in front of—adults. The process is greatly helped by Eton's tutorial system, under which small groups of boys spend time with a master every week in freewheeling discussions known as "private business."

We talked to three boys who were planning to go into the Guards. One of them said he had family connections with the Cold-

stream Guards going back to Charles II's time; another's grandfather had fought in the Welsh Guards in the First World War.

Why do they like the Guards? "Well, they certainly are the elite of the infantry," says one, "and they are a very close-knit bunch, which is rather nice. My mother, as soon as she discovered I was a boy, put me down for the regiment." Another boy, who plans to go to university first, says that the previous summer he had been with a Guards regiment in Berlin and liked what he saw. Also, since then, he adds, "My father has made his intentions quite clear."

Representatives from the different Guards' regiments visit the school each year. "Of course," says one boy, "you have to prove yourself before they will have you. It's unfortunate, this 'Eton and the Guards' image, if it keeps good people who were not here or in any public school from getting in. But the system seems to work well as it is, and there seems no point in changing it."

Another says, "Regimental headquarters told us we will not need a private income. Perhaps they still do in the Household Cavalry, but not in the Foot Guards. I think the ceremonial duties will be fun to do for a bit, but not for too long. They shouldn't be cut out because as the Earl of Mountbatten said, the best troops on the parade ground are the best on the battlefield."

[Comment: "The days have long since passed when it was an advantage to have been educated at Eton." Eric Anderson, Headmaster-Designate, in "Sayings of the Week," *The Observer*, January, 1980.]

Welcome to the Brigade Squad: A Word from your Chief Instructor

Seventeen young men, aged between eighteen and twenty-three, have been marched into a lecture room by a bristling Scots Guards sergeant—their scourge, guide, taskmaster, and mentor for the next two months. The recruits, who come mainly from the great public schools of England—Eton, Marlborough, Winchester, Wellington,

Young Etonian destined for the Welsh Guards (opposite page)

Stowe, and so on—and include two scions of the aristocracy, are red-faced and sweating from their exertions on the square. They have been in the British army for twenty-four hours.

A Guards major, Pirbright's chief instructor, walks in and goes up to the lectern. There is a demoniacal shriek from the back of the room: "*SQUAD!*" Seventeen backs go rigid in their seats and thirty-four arms shoot down the sides of the chairs, fists lightly curled, thumbs down and pressing hard on the rest of the hand to keep the elbow locked straight. "Thank you, Sergeant," the Major says. The Sergeant's contorted mouth returns, as if by magic, to a human shape.

"In my joining instructions," the Major begins, "I made a point of telling you to be fit, and I hope for your sake you *are* fit, otherwise you are going to be fairly pained during the next few weeks. Now, you'll do a certain amount of shooting on the SLR, that's the rifle, also on the GPMG, that's the submachine gun. Towards the end of your eight-week course you will do the march and shoot, which consists of a march, the assault course, and a shoot on the range. You'll do current affairs to try to keep you up to date with what's going on in the world. You'll do command tasks on the assault course, you'll do lecturettes, discussion periods, some sport, one week's exercise on Salisbury Plain, and you'll have leave, you'll be delighted to hear, at nine-thirty on October eleventh until eleven o'clock at night on October fourteeth. That's twenty-four hours more than Brigade Squads have had in the past. So much for what you will be doing in general." The Major looks around. To describe the audience as captive would be a gross understatement.

"The aim of the Brigade Squad," he continues, "is basically three things. Firstly, to show you the life of a recruit in the Household Division at its most basic. This should help you enormously, if you are lucky enough to get commissioned, to understand your men and what they have gone through before they join their regiment. Secondly, it is to prepare you for the Regular Commissions Board, and lastly, to teach you basic skills that should help you when you go forward to the Military Academy at Sandhurst.

"While you are here you will come into contact with recruits in the Navy, Army, and Air Force Institute (NAAFI), around the camp and so on. I urge you where possible to try to talk to them, try and find out what they think about life, what they think about the Guards' depot, the regiment they are going to, and so on. It is all part of your military education, of *understanding* the men you are going to command in the future. In eight weeks we *basically*, and that's very basically, try and aim for the Brigade Squad to reach a standard that

40.

a recruit would reach in twenty weeks. Now, this sounds *horrific*, but it isn't. If your instructors tell you to do a thing, we only expect them to tell you once and it gets done. With recruits we have to tell them six or seven times.

"You've probably heard of the low pass rates in previous Brigade Squads recently. The reason why so many people failed is that they were *just not up to the standard*. It's as simple as that." The Major looks around the room, a pointed, searching glance. "I certainly hope that we will get back up to our normal pass rate of seventy-five percent."*

He is talking about the Regular Commissions Board (RCB), the three-day gauntlet at a Georgian mansion in Wiltshire that all aspiring officers have to run successfully before they can enter Sandhurst. Most candidates go straight to the RCB testing ground with little or no military experience. However, the Guards, the Royal Green Jackets, and the cavalry give their potential officers two months basic training before sending them off. The principal question in the minds of the examiners is still, "Can this man command a platoon in battle?"

"The course here is *tough*," the Major says to what he admits is his seventh Brigade Squad. "It will be hard on you physically and hard on you mentally. We push you, we push you hard. We get you up at six in the morning and you get to bed at eleven at night. During those hours your feet will hardly touch the ground. . . . It is really a case of putting mind over matter.

"When you are feeling tired, feeling sore, you want to go to sleep, you want to see Mummy again, whatever it is, just set your mind to the fact you are going to get through. Come what may, you will never give up. The course, believe it or not, is for your benefit."

The Major steps down and his place is taken by a captain, the Assistant Adjutant of the depot.

"Here is an excerpt from a Russian newspaper," he says, "of a Russian's idea of a British army officer.

" 'He is a rich landowner,' " he reads, " 'house owner, capitalist or merchant, and only an officer incidentally. He knows absolutely nothing about the army and the army only sees him on parades and reviews. From the professional point of view he is the most ignorant in Europe. He does not enter the army to serve, only for the uniform and the glitter. The English uniforms are truly magnificent, cut to fit very tight. The officer has the right to consider himself

---

*The Major was not disappointed. When we later returned to Pirbright, fourteen of the seventeen had passed RCB and were going to Sandhurst.

irresistible to the fair-haired, blued-eyed misses and ladies. The English officer is an aristocrat, extremely rich, an independent sybarite and epicure. He has a spoilt, capricious, and blasé character, loves pornographic literature, suggestive pictures, recherché food, strong and strange drinks. His chief amusements are gambling, racing, and sport. He goes to bed at dawn and gets up at midday. He is usually occupied with two mistresses simultaneously, a lady of high society and a girl drawn from the ballet or opera. His income runs into several thousands, often tens of thousands a year, of which he keeps no account, being totally incapable of doing so. . . .' "

The Brigade Squad relaxed a little during this dated version of the Russian's view of the British army's officer corps. But now they are tense again.

"I would just like to say something about the standards of the Household Division," the Captain continues. "We have got tremendously high standards to maintain. First, we are going to get you fit. Then we'll give you command tasks to do . . . the sort of thing where you have to use a logical mind to work out a problem. You've got two planks and a gap, the planks are six foot long and the gap is seven foot. How are you going to get across—that sort of thing. We'll help you think logically on that. You get ten days of field training, which is to practice you in command under field conditions and instill a sense of purpose and the ability to suffer hardship. A lot of you haven't suffered any hardship in your lives. We're going to give you pride in your own regiments and you'll have your regimental histories rammed down your throats. This will give you pride in your regiments. Overall, we hope to improve your confidence by putting you on your feet and letting you talk to the rest of the group here.

"I don't think there is anything more to say except to wish you the best of luck and if you put everything into it you'll get a lot out of it, and you'll have the support of the staff all the time if you work hard. If you *don't,* watch out!"

The Captain leaves the room. Another banshee scream. "*SQUAD!*" Seventeen spines stretch to the ceiling.

"Permission to carry on please, sir?" says the Sergeant. "Carry on please, Sergeant," replies the Captain. (Field Marshal Lord Carver once asked a Guards NCO what would happen if he refused to grant such permission. "We'd carry on just the same, sir," the NCO said without batting an eye.)

The big swing in full battle-kit: the Guards notorious assault course at Pirbright (opposite page)

The Assault Course

The Major mentioned the assault course. It is discreetly hidden away, not far from the rifle range, in a copse of pine trees and heather. The ground is sandy, but it quickly turns to mud when it rains. There are thirty-one obstacles of varying difficulty and deceptiveness spread over a half-mile circuit. The soldiers are dressed in battle kit (minus headgear) and carry packs weighing between thirty and thirty-five pounds. To make sure the weight is correct, the NCO's obligingly pour sand into the Guardsmen's ammunition pouches. Each man also carries his rifle, almost another ten pounds, and one poor recruit is lumbered with the machine gun, another twenty-seven pounds. The official time for the course is fifteen minutes for an individual and twenty-two minutes for a section of eight men.

Recruits who have been in the army for three months are clustered under the trees at the beginning of the course. They spread out in a realistic tactical deployment, flat on their stomachs, covering each other with their rifles. They have to do this between each obstacle, notionally protecting the last men coming over. The sergeant in charge taps the magazine of his rifle with a bayonet and they are off.

Some of the obstacles are relatively easy—low walls, moderate jumps, and so on. Others, like the twenty-foot-high scramble net, the ten-foot wall, and the jungle ropes across water, are simply terrifying. The remainder fall into the category of looking like a cinch but suddenly and exhaustingly proving the opposite. They are the worst of all. The secret is teamwork. "We're not interested in one man getting the Victoria Cross," says the Sergeant. "We're interested in *eight* men getting it."

The Guardsmen know the course well but still find it hard going. The Sergeant is everywhere at once, a lean wiry man as fit as a fiddle, determined to improve the section's performance. "Smith," he yells to one of the recruits who is swinging over a dirty-looking trough of water, "keep your bloody mouth shut or you'll bloody drink that water." Another big lad, carrying the machine gun, his face contorted with strain, falls short on the Tarzan ropes and crashes into the cold, muddy water. He scrambles out, is sent back, and leaps into the air. His feet touch dry land on the other side, but he doesn't have enough momentum. For a moment he teeters, trying desperately to hurl himself forward as his comrades reach out to grab him. But gravity wins, and he topples backward with another resounding splash.

44.

Hanging on. "Nothing to it," the Sergeant says (opposite page)
Before and after. "Second to None" (pages 46–47)

Farther along there are a series of concrete pipes about three feet in diameter. They are placed on a slope facing uphill. The aim is to crawl through them, and it looks easy enough. Unfortunately, the concrete pipes are in the "cinch" category. It is one of the most exhausting of all the tasks, even when you know how to do it. The secret is to crawl into the pipe, turn on your back, and drag yourself up to the other end by pulling and pushing with your arms. The rub is that you are going uphill—that's what takes the juice out of you.

The "monkey bars," a series of rectangular iron bars eight feet off the ground and extending over about thirty feet of water, also look pretty harmless. You simply swing from hand to hand and emerge dry and triumphant at the other end. The Sergeant cons the writer into having go. "Nothing to it," the Sergeant says. A couple of minutes later there is a yell and another splash. It takes a swift and polished performance by the photographer, who goes hand-over-hand as if Jane were waiting for him at the other end, to restore some semblance of dignity to the team.

The Guardsmen face their second eight-foot wall and begin to swarm over it. The Sergeant and the platoon officer, a young ensign, yell at them but also give encouragement and praise. Occasionally they leap over the obstacles themselves to show, in the time-honored fashion, that anything a Guardsman can do they can do as well, or even better. All of the training staff at Pirbright are required to keep fit and go round the assault course at regular intervals to keep their hand in.

The last jump of all is a deceptive one. There is a ramp rising to about six feet off the ground, followed by a six-foot-wide ditch. The problem is that you only see the ditch when you reach the top of the ramp and are already in mid-stride. Knowing it is there doesn't seem to help very much to gauge its true width. It is a fitting end to one of the world's toughest assault courses, and the soldiers who have just negotiated it in a respectable time collapse on the ground for a well-earned smoke. It is then we discover that they have already been around the course once that afternoon. Fifteen minutes later they will be doing it all over again.

"It's bloody murder," says a Guards sergeant who trained with the New Zealand army's special forces and came away convinced that the Pirbright assault course was considerably harder than anything he had had to face out there. The assault course is an integral part of the Guardsman's final test, which he must do before he passes out of the depot and joins his regiment. This is known as the Commandant's "March and Shoot" and it consists of a three-mile run across country with full equipment (thirty-five-pound packs and ten-pound rifles), a two-minute break, the assault course, another two-minute break, and then accurate battle shooting on the rifle range. The run must be completed in thirty-four minutes and the assault course completed in twenty-two minutes.

Anyone who visits the Pirbright assault course will, sooner or later, hear the story of the U.S. Marines. There are two versions that have passed into Guards mythology. The first has the Marines coming to inspect it when they were redesigning their own course. Two of the obstacles immediately struck them as being unacceptable, and they also considered the whole thing much too long. They went back home and built a shorter, easier course. The other version describes a group of visiting Marines being invited to have a go. The Americans, the story runs, took one look at it and shook their heads. "No thanks," they said politely.

The Old Boy Net

"Once a Guardsman, always a Guardsman," they say, and there is a lot of truth in it. The Guards, more than most, look after their own. The Household Division is full of official, semiofficial, and unofficial organizations that raise money, select officers, guide promotions, find jobs, look after the indigent, endow chapels and memorials, campaign against regimental reductions or amalgamations, and minimize scandals.

The most important organizations are the seven regimental headquarters, all located in London. The Guards regimental headquarters are much more active and involved in the lives of their regiments than those of the infantry and cavalry regiments of the line. Headed by the "Lieutenant Colonel commanding the Regiment," who, with usual Guards logic, is a full colonel, the headquarters have developed a high degree of autonomy, and it is to them, rather than to army hierarchy itself, that officers and NCO's in the Division look for promotions, postings, and guidance.

These headquarters, run by a small but busy staff and festooned with pictures and memorabilia of the regiment's corporate life, perform a vital function in the Guards' existence. They are at one and the same time museum, record office, personnel management office, welfare organization, show-business agency, social club, treasury, and publishing house. Their most important work is the selection of officers, the promotion of NCO's and the shaping of their careers. Nothing, however, is too trivial for their attention. "If a painting falls off

Former Garrison Sergeant Major Taylor, Grenadier Guards, door-keeping at the House of Lords (page 50)
Guardsman Moxon, ex-Coldstream Guards, now a Chelsea Pensioner (page 51)

the wall in the officers' mess in Germany," said a member of the Grenadier Guards regimental headquarters, "they will turn to us."

The daily routine of a regimental headquarters will find itself involved in things like checking the births column in the *Times* and sending out letters to former members of the regiment who have just produced a son. A young man who has recently left school and expressed an interest in becoming an officer in the regiment will be interviewed. An officer has applied to go on a course and headquarters has to decide whether he should. Sandhurst or another training institution wants two drill instructors from the regiment: can they be spared, and who should go? A senior NCO, a good chap, is due to leave the army soon. Does anyone know of a job that might suit him? The Queen's Birthday Parade (Trooping the Color) is coming up, and the regiment will be allotted a number of tickets for distribution among families and friends. A record company is interested in the regimental band making a new record: how should the royalties be divided? It is time for someone from the headquarters to visit the Old Comrades Associations in the Manchester area. And a charming letter arrived this morning from an old lady in Birmingham whose husband was killed in the First World War and whose son was killed in the Second. Both served in the regiment, but now, alas, she has fallen on hard times. Can the regiment help her out? A Guardsman has been killed in Northern Ireland. His body has to be flown home, his family notified, compensation worked out. Recruiting figures are down, but the summer is coming so it is time to put the regimental recruiting team on the road again in their four-ton vehicle towing a large trailer.

And down at the Depot the batch that came in on that marvelous Indian summer day five months ago is due to pass out as full-fledged Guardsmen. The Grenadiers make a point of sending each new member of the regiment a certificate showing the Queen's Company Color, the Royal Standard of the Regiment. Under the rubric "The First or Grenadier Regiment of Foot Guards" it says, "This is to certify that . . . . is serving his Queen and country as a Guardsman in the Grenadier Guards."

53.

Timothy Tufnell, MC, former major, Grenadier Guards, at Bucks Club, London (opposite page)

Sandhurst

It is a lovely, misty, quintessentially English spring day. The sun has broken through the clouds and warms the parade ground, where a dress rehearsal is about to take place. Three weeks from now, in front of proud parents and military dignitaries, the Sovereign's Parade will be staged in glorious Technicolor, accompanied by martial music. The sword of honor will be presented to the best cadet and "Auld Lang Syne" will fill the summery air as the Academy's adjutant rides his charger up the steps and through the doors of Old College.

Situated on the Surrey-Berkshire border, Sandhurst is a fine piece of eighteenth-century parkland spread over a generous 650 acres. There are good trees, gracious lawns recovering from the winter blight, and biscuit-colored and red-brick buildings set at discreet distances from each other. There is a stream with stepping stones and a lake constructed by French prisoners during the Napoleonic Wars. It is a place remembered with affection and nostalgia by military men in Britain and around the world. Generals, politicians, kings and princes, bishops, playwrights, lawyers and teachers—men of all races, creeds, and colors have passed through the wrought-iron gates that first swung open in 1812.

And the people they probably recall most vividly are the noncommissioned officers who trained them, especially the drill instructors who marched them up and down on the hallowed square. Unlike St. Cyr and West Point, the French and American equivalents, a major part of instruction at Sandhurst is left to the NCO's, and of these the largest contingent are men from the Household Division. The two most important jobs in the Academy—the Adjutant and the Academy Sergeant Major—are *always* held by Guardsmen.

The star, by common consent, is the Academy Sergeant Major, the most senior NCO in the British army. Not only is he a man of great experience and perfect poise, but he usually also has such qualities as wit, understanding, and style. He is called "Sir" by the other NCO's and by the cadets, and he deserves it. His tenure is long—ten years is not uncommon—and his impact, especially on the parade ground, where he reigns supreme, is something generations of officers never forget.

The Academy Sergeant Major we met was a tall, striking Grenadier Guardsman. Before his cadets come on parade, he says, he

Academy Sergeant Major Huggins, Grenadier Guards (opposite page)
Sandhurst cadets rehearsing for their passing-out parade (pages 56–57)
Preserving it all for their grandchildren (pages 58–59)

likes them to be "clean, shaved, and lightly oiled." He stands now in front of a microphone and reviews the rehearsal. He tells the cadets it wasn't too bad, better than the last one, but still not good enough. "Believe it or not," he barks, "there are still people marching off on the wrong foot. If I were you, I would fall on my bayonet."

The relationship between the NCO's at Sandhurst and the young men they train to become their superiors is a curious one. Contempt, affection, pity and pride are all present, but somehow, like an improbable recipe that unexpectedly produces a delicious dish, the mixture seems to work. The army clearly believes it is the best way, for, although there have been many changes at Sandhurst over the years, particularly since the Second World War, the preeminence of the Guards' NCO's has been questioned but not seriously challenged.

What goes on at the personal level between instructor and instructed is another matter. While most NCO's seem to be happy with the metamorphosis they have wrought in the young men in their charge, there is the occasional exception. A case in point was a cadet who later became a leading political figure in Britain. The day before he passed out he was called over by his platoon sergeant. "Tomorrow, Bloggs," the NCO said, "you will be an officer and I will be saluting you and calling you Sir." Pause. "However, I want you to know that deep down I will always think of you as a cunt."

These days Sandhurst is not a very academic place. Career officers' time there has been cut from two years to a year, half of it being devoted almost entirely to military skills. Short-service officers who sign on for a three-year stint in the army spend only six months at the Academy. West Point, which provides a four-year course for all its cadets, combines military training with academic although it stresses the latter. "A second-rate university with a first-rate cadet corps," says the Academy Sergeant Major a little unkindly.

But why should the Guards play such a dominant role at Sandhurst and, inevitably, inculcate the army's officer corps with something of their own ideas and standards?

The Academy's adjutant, a fit-looking Scots Guards major with a large black Labrador under his desk, explains.

"The question is raised virtually every year," he says, "but it has been proved that NCO's from other regiments cannot do the job. They simply did not have that magical ability to control, command, instruct, and get the best out of potential officers. I'm not saying one of the others can't do it—Guards NCO's do not occupy every platoon position—but on the whole they can't. The net result was let's not rock the boat, the system is working, so leave it alone."

The End of the Road: The Royal Hospital

The scarlet coat, cocked hat, and chest full of medals of the Chelsea Pensioner is as familiar a sight in London as the Guards themselves. Situated close to the Thames, the Royal Hospital is a memorial not only to Sir Christopher Wren's architectural genius but also to his compassion. He built it as a home for old soldiers, a function it still faithfully serves today, more than three centuries later. When the chapel was being constructed Wren stipulated that no stained glass be used in the windows, so that the old men "could see the sky."

It is a comfortable and happy refuge for former NCO's and men of other ranks who are over sixty-five years of age and who have nowhere else to go. It is organized on military lines in six companies, with pensioners serving as company sergeant majors. Each man has his own room, uniform, and a small allowance. The food is good, there is a heavily patronized bar—run on the lines of a pub—and, in general, the atmosphere of sprightly gaiety about the whole place is a pleasure to behold.

Former Guardsmen, ranging in age from an infantile seventy to a respectable eighty-six, have gathered to chat and have their photographs taken. There is a tendency for some of them to talk at once while a few say nothing at all; one very old boy falls asleep almost immediately.

A tall Scots Guardsman with a waxed mustache—he is one of the hospital's company sergeant majors—bristles at the delay. "Get on with it then," he says, "I'm a busy man." Another, almost as grumpy, says he has a lot of telephone calls to make. A third says he has a "date."

"Once a Grenadier, never again," says a Grenadier Guardsman turning the popular saw on its head. He joined the army in 1914 and was paid sixpence (equivalent to 2½ p, or about five cents, today) a week as a boy soldier. "I fled to the army," says an octogenarian Coldstreamer who enlisted in 1912. "I was an orphan, you see. It was very rough, especially for the boy soldiers. Lashings with rifle slings were quite common in those days. The army was the scum of the services. It was amazing what some people did to get out of it. I remember an Irish Guardsman who went out on guard wearing two right boots. To prove he was insane, you see."

A group is selected to have their pictures taken in the cloisters. When the camera starts to click someone says "cheese" and a muffled voice comes from the back—"My Gawd, I haven't got my teeth in." During a short break a diminutive old man, dressed in the pensioners' everyday blue uniform and peaked forage cap, walks by carrying a large brown paper bag. As he does so he raises his cane and shouts, "Stick it in your ear!"

Later we are shown the dining-room table where the Duke of Wellington was laid out after he died; a brass plaque marks the exact spot. And then, at the invitation of three old comrades who served together in the Coldstream Guards in the early twenties, we adjourn to the pensioners' warm, smokey, oak-paneled pub.

For the sake of convenience we'll call the trio Fred, Bert, and Arthur. Fred joined the Coldstream Guards on April 13, 1920, as a drummer boy and stayed in the army until 1943, when he was wounded in Italy and invalided out. He rattles off his army number—in the way that all old soldiers can do—to show that almost forty years of civilian life have not dimmed his memory. He is a small man with glasses, a bit nutty, but funny and sharp-witted. He claims a relative on his mother's side came over with William the Conqueror. Untypically, he doesn't drink. Nor, he says, does he smoke or go out with women. He also claims he has a healthy bank balance. At one stage in the proceedings he nods off. "He can go to sleep on a clothesline," says Arthur, giving him an affectionate glance.

Bert, eighty-three years old but in fine shape and as articulate as an actor, drinks a steady stream of whiskies with a little water. He has nine grandchildren and ten great-grandchildren. He fought throughout the entire 1914–18 War—"the great war of civilization," he says with a sniff—and was never wounded or gassed. He did have one miraculous escape but is reluctant to recount the story, since, he says, it is so bizarre that few people believe him. But, after a few whiskies, he tells it anyway.

"It was during the battle of Loos," he says. "The Germans were counterattacking, and I felt a sudden blow in my ear as I fired at them. There was no blood, but I didn't have time to check any further until after the battle. There was something wrong with my rifle, and when I looked at it I noticed there was a small hole in the wooden stock near the muzzle. I turned it in to the armorer. He checked it over and then turned to me and said, "You're a lucky man." He held up the rifle and showed me another small hole in the stock at the butt end. The bullet had gone clean through the stock and whistled out past my bloody ear!"

62.

A quiet moment for an old Guardsman in Christopher Wren's Royal Hospital, Chelsea (opposite page)
Chelsea Pensioners in their favorite pub, the bar of the Royal Hospital (pages 64–65)
"You won't see a sad face among us" (pages 66–67)

Major General
George Salis Schwabe C.B.
Colonel 3rd Dragoon Guards.
He served in the Carabiniers and
16th Lancers which latter Regiment
he commanded for four years.
He took part in the Zulu War
and commanded the troops in
Mauritius.
Lieutenant-Governor
of this Hospital for seven years
from 1898 to 1905.
Died June 13th 1907, aged 63.
This Tablet is placed here by his Wife.

To the memory of
Colonel Richard Wadeson, V.C.
Major and Lieutenant Governor of this
Hospital from 1881 to 1885.
Previously for thirty-five years in Her
Majesty's 75th (Stirlingshire) Regiment
now the 1st Battalion of the Gordon
Highlanders, passing through all grades to
the command of the Regiment.
Died in the Hospital 26 January 1885
Age 58 years.
This Tablet is erected by the Board of
Commissioners of the Hospital on behalf
of the In Pensioners as a record of their
affection and respect.

Arthur is in his seventies and ended his army career as a quartermaster captain, but he dropped rank to enter the Royal Hospital. He says he has never regretted it. He doesn't wear his medals any more when he goes out into the King's Road, not since a small boy came up to him and said, "Hey governor, what did you get them broaches for?" Like many Guardsmen, he used to play pranks to relieve the boredom of ceremonial duties. Once, he says, he bound up the hammer of the clock in the Tower of London with a pair of puttees. When the clock should have struck the hour all it produced was a dull thump. "I forgot I had my army number on the puttees and I finished up in detention in Chelsea Barracks."

The men in the bar are, in a sense, back in the military cradle with the army once again assuming the parental role. It's almost as if their intervening lives had never happened. These old soldiers have given up their relatives, their pensions, their freedom to come into the Hospital where they will remain in the brotherhood of the barrack-room until they die. They have achieved an improbable though blissful state of military grace where parades are optional, dignity is bestowed without duty and where the uniform is a daily reminder of individual service rather than collective subordination.

Arthur pauses and looks around at the animated scene, the rows of golden pint pots of beer on the trestle tables and blue smoke curling up to the molded ceiling. He raises his third pint to his lips. "What is lovely about all this," he says with pride, "is that you won't see a sad face among us."

Some of The Colors and Standards of the Household Division, Guards Chapel, London

Part II

Pomp
and
Circumstance

Military Show Business: Trooping the Color

*"The better you dress a soldier,
the more highly will he be thought of by the women
and, consequently, by himself."*
—*Field Marshal Lord Wolseley,*
The Soldier's Pocketbook *(1914–18 War)*

The crowds are beginning to gather in the Mall. It is the usual mixture found in London during June—foreign tourists, families in from the suburbs or the country, groups of students, and a few old couples who sound like native Londoners. Today, however, there is also a strong leavening of men who have a military bearing inadequately disguised by their well-cut suits (handkerchiefs, *de rigueur*, in top pockets), trilby or bowler hats, and furled umbrellas. As if this civilian "uniform" were not enough to identify them as a group, they are all wearing the same discreet and not very exciting tie; the navy and maroon stripes of the Guards.

Union Jacks with heavy gold tassels flap languidly from flagpoles spaced at regular intervals along the Mall, contrasting with the billowing green foliage of the trees behind them. Guards bandsmen, in scarlet tunics and blue trousers, are selling programs: fifty pence apiece. A Royal Parks cleaning van moves slowly toward Buckingham Palace. It will be in action later, sweeping up horse dung after the cavalry have ridden by. Banks of red and yellow tulips encircle the Victoria Memorial, superb against a backdrop of water, willows and swans in St. James's Park.

Comments come from the early-bird spectators who have staked a claim to the front rows around the Memorial and its approaches. "I come every year. . . . Marvelous show, isn't it? . . . It's tradition, roots, you know what I mean?" "The weather will be good," says one veteran, "because goslings were hatched in the Queen's park this morning." "Wouldn't miss it for the world," says another. "It's a lovely show."

Not everyone agrees. A London taxi driver is scornful. "Lot of old rubbish. Makes you sick. Little tin soldiers marching up and down trying to make out we're still something when we're really one of the lesser Common Market countries." He pauses and glances at the sky. "The Guardsmen won't bloody faint today, will they? More likely they'll get chilblains."

At the final rehearsal a week earlier, three men fainted during the parade—an officer from his horse, a lance sergeant, and a Guardsman. A knowledgeable NCO offers no explanation for the officer and the Guardsman, but he is sure about the sergeant. "He was on the pot the night before, wasn't he?" Guardsmen who suddenly fall out in this manner are a major preoccupation of the Fleet Street newspapers, which have been known to caption the event "Drooping the Color." But today it is cool and overcast, the sort of weather Guardsmen pray for, providing it doesn't rain.

Down at Chelsea Barracks the Guardsmen have been up since 6:30 a.m. They have done some vigorous physical exercises before breakfast—to warm them up and loosen their bowels—eaten a substantial meal, and spent a good hour getting their kit ready. At 8:45 they are ready for inspection and some arms drill. An hour later, timed by a stopwatch, they step off for Horse Guards.

The Household Cavalry at Knightsbridge Barracks, on a fashionable edge of Hyde Park, are up at dawn exercising their horses in the early gray light. A cavalry trooper preparing himself for one of the great ceremonial parades is not unlike a medieval knight getting ready for battle. He is not hoisted into the saddle by a crane, but putting on the buckskin breeches, sword belt, tunic, gleaming cuirass, thigh-length riding boots, spurs, white gauntlets, and plumed helmet is neither a simple nor a speedy process.

Though the ceremony of Trooping the Color to honor the sovereign's birthday dates back to 1755, the Household Cavalry have only been part of it since the end of the Second World War, when King George VI suggested they join what had until then been an exclusively Foot Guards affair. Today the cavalry are undeniably a spectacular addition. Much of their éclat is provided by their highly skilled mounted band, splendidly costumed in coats of gold, which joins the massed bands of the Foot Guards to add a fitting musical accompaniment to the visual impact of the occasion.

73.

Final preparations for the Trooping: getting used to the weight of the bearskin, Chelsea Barracks (pages 74–75)
A timed departure from Chelsea for an on-cue appearance at Horse Guards on the Queen's Birthday (pages 76–77)
The Household Cavalry at the trot (pages 78–79)

At Horse Guards in Whitehall, the center of the stage, preparations have also been going on since daybreak. Security has tightened as a result of the IRA's activities, and dogs are used to search for hidden explosives before the parade begins. Horse Guards has been the home of the Household Division since Stuart times, but the present building facing St. James's Park dates from the middle of the eighteenth century, when it was remodeled by William Kent and officially opened by King George II riding under the archway.

The scene inside the building an hour or so before the Trooping commences is not unlike the commotion backstage on the opening night of a West End or Broadway musical. There is much hustle and bustle, some controlled confusion, and a general air of expectancy and excitement. A man in dress uniform carrying a cocked hat scurries by, muttering to himself; officials in morning coats and gray toppers move purposefully through the labyrinth of eighteenth-century corridors; floors are so shiny in the rooms where the royal family will sit and watch the parade that there are signs posted warning you not to slip on them; a television crew gets lost and ends up in a toilet. Outside, ladies, dressed in heavy tweeds—ready for the hazards of sitting in the open for more than two hours in England's "blazing June"—clutch their tickets and search anxiously for their seats.

The first act, however, takes place outside Buckingham Palace. The gates open and members of the royal family are driven out in state carriages, around the Victoria Memorial—the "wedding cake" in the Guards' idiom—past the Mounted Band, and down the Mall, which now has two impeccably drawn lines of scarlet separating the pavement from the roadway. Stretching down the 1,821 yards of the avenue, are 20 officers and 428 men, 6 paces apart from each other.

All the performers pass this way—bands, cavalry, foot soldiers, horse artillery, carriages, and so on. The climax is when the Queen, Colonel-in-Chief of all the seven Household regiments, rides sidesaddle out of the gate, wearing the uniform of the regiment whose color is being "trooped" that day. The officer in charge of the detachment of Foot Guards outside the palace betrays the tension of the moment. His white-gloved hand, opens and closes nervously as he waits to give the command for the "present arms" salute. As if affected by the same jitters, a Life Guards horse stretches out its hind legs and pees mightily on the road in front of the gates. His rider, an officer, appears unconcerned and automatically moves his body forward slightly to ease the strain. Perhaps there is a drill for this. Anyway, the Royal Parks cleaning truck will be along soon.

Back at Horse Guards, the curtain is about to go up. Martial music and shouted commands can be heard from the Mall. The skirl of the bagpipes playing 'Hielan Laddie' fill the air. The clatter of horse hooves and the jingle of cavalry on the move become clearer and clearer. Slowly, methodically, rhythmically, every piece of the pageant moves into its assigned position on the Horse Guards parade ground in front of the banked rows of spectators. And then, at 11:00 a.m. precisely, as the clock above Horse Guards chimes, the Queen arrives and the parade begins.

For those watching from the stands who are neither British nor military people, the whole business may seem slightly dotty: the hoarse commands, ramrod backs, stamping feet, endless saluting, high cost, and the essential pointlessness of it all. Although they may enjoy it as a spectacle, their conclusion may be similar to that of the French general who watched the Charge of the Light Brigade, murmuring when it was all over, *"C'est magnifique, mais ce n'est pas la guerre."*

But for those who have a military bent or who feel the tug of tradition when they see a bearskin or hear "The British Grenadiers," the Trooping is a rich personal experience. Every detail has meaning. The expert will note that while the Life Guards wear scarlet tunics and white plumes on their helmets and the Blues and Royals have blue tunics and red plumes, the trumpeters in both regiments wear red plumes and ride grays, as originally ordered by King James II, who wanted them to be easily distinguishable in battle when needed to sound a call.

Even the arrangement of the Foot Guards' buttons—singly for the Grenadiers, in pairs for the Coldstream, in threes for the Scots Guards, and so on—and the color and positioning of their plumes is interesting. The gleaming axes of the farriers, the cocked hats of the quartermasters, the banging of the feet adopted by King George V, who liked it, the intricate spin wheel of the massed bands—a diverting piece of choreography in which the musicians change direction by pivoting on themselves—and the symbolism of the ceremony itself all have significance.

The Trooping ritual has its origins in medieval warfare. At that time it was crucial that every man in a regiment be able to recognize his own flag or standard—the "color"—so that he could rally around it in battle.* That primitive imperative no longer exists, and the symbolism of the ceremony is of a different sort. The Trooping

---

*For a more detailed description, see Appendix.

always takes place on the monarch's official birthday, and the parade, besides being a major tourist attraction, is a reaffirmation of the House-hold Division's loyalty and links to the sovereign. "It's our way of saying happy birthday to her," says a Grenadier Guards officer. "The crowds, the photographers, and the rest don't really exist. It's just us and the monarch." A Coldstream Guards NCO says the same thing in a different way. "She's the top soldier. . . . It's 'er troops what are on parade. It's 'er day."

There is a moment, near the end of the ceremony, when the Queen rides amidst her Guards along the Mall back to the palace, that can touch the hearts of aficionados and skeptics alike. The best place to see it is from the Victoria Memorial. Here you find the veteran photographers who have covered the parade a dozen times, armed with huge lenses that look like small artillery pieces and precise topograph-ical knowledge of where to place the tripod and how to angle the camera. They also know what the weather is supposed to do. A dull sky is no bad thing for contrast with the brilliance of the martial colors. But at the magical moment when the Queen, a solitary yet cosseted rider in the center of the phalanx of marching men that fills the entire Mall, comes into focus, the sun should send a silvery shaft of light down on her.

On this occasion, it did, illuminating not only her small tidy figure on horseback but the breastplates of the cavalry, the brass and silver of the musicians' instruments, the scarlet, gold and white of the uniforms, the glossy flanks of the horses, the sea of swaying bearskins, and, not least, the soft natural greens, grays, and roses of the ancient stone and incomparable parklands of London.

Tricks of the Trade

The Guards' ceremonial duties—the trooping, changing the guard at the royal palaces, providing escorts for foreign dignitaries, attending the state opening of Parliament, and so on—are familiar sights. But how is each show put together? Is it as simple as it looks? What are the pitfalls and how are they avoided?

As with all good theater—continuing the metaphor—the Guards have skilled and dedicated performers, a good script, adequate financial backing, and a willingness to rehearse and rehearse until the thing is perfect.

The most important men are the Guards drill instructors, who serve as producers, directors, and actors all rolled into one, under the overall command of the Garrison Sergeant Major, the highest-ranking noncommissioned officer in London. The script is simple. Everything to do with public duties is contained in a large book called *Household Division Standing Orders*, the Guards' ceremonial "bible."

Guards begin their ceremonial training from the moment they enter the army at the depot in Pirbright. Sentry boxes sit on the side of the square, and a section of the road that runs through the camp is regularly converted into the "Mall" to train the troops who will line the real thing in London later on. The officers' training, especially sword drill, is also in the hands of the drill instructors, and rank becomes unimportant as captains or majors practice under the critical eye of a color sergeant.

In all public duties, timing is a delicate matter. When the Guardsmen step off from Chelsea Barracks during the Trooping, an NCO times their departure with a stopwatch. The distance to Horse Guards is known to the foot, but crucial minutes may be gained—or lost—en route if an unforeseen event, like a road accident, interrupts the even rhythm of the march.

The arrival of the Queen at Horse Guards at the stroke of eleven is often regarded as a minor miracle, since she has ridden more than a mile from Buckingham Palace. It wasn't always as straightforward as it is now. The chimes of the clock used to be adjusted to meet her arrival, but when a BBC commentator gave the game away the Queen insisted that it should never happen again.

Fainting on parade is a recurrent nightmare for all Guardsmen, including officers. It doesn't often happen in cool weather, but when the temperature goes up the risks increase. The most common cause of collapse is an overtight headband inside the bearskin or helmet that becomes an instrument of torture as the head swells in the heat.

Onlookers peering through the railings of Buckingham Palace often wonder how the two sentries know when to step out of their boxes and begin their measured, perfectly synchronized patrol. It is done with a series of taps of the rifle butt on the ground and finger signs, with the right-hand sentry as you face them—always the senior man of the pair—giving the cue.

One tap of the rifle on the ground means a patrol, two are for an ordinary salute, three for a "present arms," and a couple of double taps warn that a patrol is coming to inspect the sentries or relieve them. When the sentries are marching and can see each other, finger signals are used: one outstretched finger means "halt and stand at ease," two fingers indicate a salute or patrol, and three fingers signify "present arms."

91.

Inspection. Corps of Drums of the Irish Guards, Wellington Barracks (pages 92-93)
The final word for the Blues and Royals at Knightsbridge Barracks before they mount The Queen's Life Guard in Whitehall (pages 94–95)

Guardsmen at the royal palaces are not issued live ammunition, but a supply is kept in the guardroom. Normal security is the responsibility of the police, but these days the Guards do "tactical" patrolling at night wearing rubber boots and forage caps instead of bearskins, and equipped with two-way radios. However, if they bumped into the Queen on their rounds they would give her the "present arms" salute.

There is much backstage work done on the uniforms. Guards NCO's insist on having the peaks of their forage caps doctored by regimental tailors to make them lie flatter on the nose. It certainly makes the wearer look more formidable, although it tends to obscure his vision. (Critics of the Guards would say that doesn't much matter, since they are already a blinkered breed.) Officers bend the crown of their caps down at the sides to make them look worn in, and no one likes to be seen with a *new* Sam Browne belt.

The King's Troop, Royal Horse Artillery, which is not part of the Household Division although it performs ceremonial duties, adopted the practice of wearing women's nylon tights beneath their breeches to prevent unseemly wrinkling. The Household Cavalry apparently use similar stratagems, though no one would admit that he actually wore tights.

There are, it seems, no great secrets about how to control a horse on parade. The animal should be well exercised that morning, the rider accustomed to his steed, and at no time should anything ever be taken for granted. "You must *ride* your nag every moment," said one of the seasoned cavalry officers. "It can be fatal if you just sit there and relax."

Accidents, when they happen, tend to occur when a Foot Guards officer finds himself in the saddle. There was a famous incident when a Coldstream officer missed his scabbard as he was trying to sheath his sword and jabbed the horse's rump instead. The animal took off down the Mall as if it were in the last straight of the Derby, with the unfortunate infanteer pulling unavailingly on the reins, his bearskin askew and his sword clenched between his teeth.

Apart from the weight of his equipment and the unpredictability of his mount, the Household Cavalryman suffers another disability—his helmet. If it is not adjusted correctly it can slip down onto the bridge of his nose—it doesn't have far to go—and commence sawing it in two. The hazard is the same whether you are a Life Guard and wear the brass chin stay—"curb chain" in the Foot Guards—under the lower lip or a Blue and Royal and wear it under the chin.

There is also the question of visibility. "I remember the first time I took part in Trooping the Color," Lord Mountbatten of Burma and former Colonel of the Life Guards once said. "At the end of the parade, which I thought was very good, I said to the Queen, 'Very good parade.' Whereupon Prince Philip turned round and said, 'How the hell do you know? You can't see a damned thing under that hat.' He was quite right, you can't."

There is one area that is much more hazardous for the Guards than for the average performer: coping with an importunate audience. The sentries who used to be stationed outside the gates of Buckingham Palace were so harassed that they were eventually placed out of harm's way inside the forecourt. But the sentries at St. James's Palace and at Windsor Castle are still exposed to the public.

The irony of the Guards having to be guarded is a painful one, but on some occasions the harassment becomes so great that an officer or an NCO has to intervene. "It's all right when a pretty girl is pinning her name and address on your bayonet," said a Guardsman, "but most of the time the tourists are a bloody nuisance."

The approved hiding place for a note of assignation, according to the Guardsmen, is the bayonet scabbard if you are in the Foot Guards, or inside the riding boot if you are a cavalryman. Guardsmen admit that when the right sort of girl comes along, there is some compensation for the trouble they are given by the public. An NCO in Berlin, reminiscing about his time on ceremonial duties, said, "They love the uniform and tell you to bring it around when you go over to their place. Well, you can't wear it off duty so you bung it into a suitcase and put it on when you get there. Mind you," he murmured, "you're not in it for long."

No show is complete without music, and the Guards have plenty of that—five regimental bands and the pipes and drums of the Foot Guards and the mounted band of the Household Cavalry. During the Trooping ceremony there are more than three hundred musicians on parade, and even the daily guard-mounting ceremony never has less than forty-five men playing their hearts out.

Men who join the Guards bands become, in effect, professional musicians. When they enlist in the army they do only six weeks basic training and then begin their musical careers, first at the Guards depot and later at the Royal Military School of Music. Recently, they have all taken courses to qualify as medical assistants, a job they would be expected to perform in wartime, but the rest of their military life is devoted to music and ceremony.

In addition to playing at all the major ceremonial occasions, the Guards bands also regale the guests at state banquets—a number of their musicians double as string players—perform at concerts, go on extended tours, and make long-playing records.

The new Guard prepares to march from Chelsea to Buckingham Palace in greatcoats (pages 98–99)
Band of the Coldstream Guards marching from Wellington Barracks for a winter Guard change (pages 100–101)

Guards bandsmen are allowed to teach and perform outside their military duties. Guardsmen have been hired as extras and part-time musicians in London's most popular theaters since the eighteenth century, and the practice continues today.

"We're like a business in a sense," said one regimental director of music. "While the government pays for our uniforms, we buy our own instruments. We turn over at least sixty thousand pounds a year and are more or less self-supporting. A percentage of our earnings goes back to the government, another slice goes to the band fund, and the rest is divided up among the musicians."

Is there any difference between a Guards band and other fine military bands? "You can always tell a Guards band when you play a record," says the same director of music. "Don't ask me why . . . there's something about a Guards band. You can tell it from the trombones. The tone is assimilated by each new generation of musicians. They absorb what has been handed down. They are, of course, the very best."

While the Foot Guards rotate between ceremonial and operational duties, the Household Cavalry maintain a permanent unit in Knightsbridge Barracks to cope with their share of public duties. Known as the Mounted Regiment, the unit is composed of a squadron each from the Life Guards and Blues and Royals. Ceremonial is a full-time job for these men, though they rotate with members of their parent regiments in Windsor and in Detmold, Germany.

A brief visit to Knightsbridge reveals that the men of the Mounted Regiment are not underemployed. Two hundred and fifty horses—all from Ireland—and the "state kit" that is piled upon rider and mount take a lot of looking after. There is also a continuous round of training and exercising that means a busy life even when the demands of ceremony are slack.

On a cold April morning troopers are lining up for inspection before they ride down to Horse Guards. An officer and the regimental Corporal Major—there are no sergeants in the cavalry—walk along the ranks of riders as troopers in khaki fatigues give man and beast the finishing touches—a dab of polish here, a wipe with a rag there.

The sound of hammering and the stench of singed hoof come from the forge. Inside are a couple of cavalry blacksmiths clad in red singlets and leather aprons, oblivious to the raw cold. Horses have to be reshod every month—a thousand shoes—which keeps the smithies in their medieval surroundings busy.

Also inside the barracks there is a riding school where skittish young remounts are allowed to run free and shake the stiffness out of their joints. The riding master, a major and two NCO's crack their whips, and the young horse sails over the jumps. When they think he has had enough, the major taps the handle of his whip against a bucket of oats. The horse, dancing lightly around the ring, turns on a penny and trots over, nostrils flared and ears up.

Once a year, usually in September, the Mounted Regiment is released from its ceremonial yoke and goes off for a three-week summer camp in a stretch of meadowland not far from Pirbright. The ride down takes six hours down the motorway and, the cavalrymen say, the horses love it. Everyone lives under canvas, and the scene, with the horse lines, tented camp, men on the move in worn riding boots and khaki breeches, the bugler blowing reveille in the misty dawn, and the occasional patrician car—a Bentley or an old Armstrong Siddeley perhaps—parked under the trees, is reminiscent of a distant, Kiplingesque era.

The clothing of a Guards officer maintains a small but thriving world of military tailors and their support troops—the clothmakers, embroiderers, hatmakers, bootmakers, swordmakers, and so on. There are three official tailors for the Household Division: Rogers, John Jones and Johns & Pegg, both in Clifford Street, and Meyer & Mortimer in Sackville Street. They are, of course, civilian tailors too, but a large part of their work is tied up with the esoteric business of ceremonial uniforms.

The tailors make regular trips to Sandhurst to measure the young gentlmen for their No. 1 dress (Blue Patrol), which they have to pay for themselves out of their clothing allowance. The "state kit"— scarlet tunic, sword belt, and so on—is issued to them by the regimental quartermaster secondhand or is made specially for them by the military tailors. All ceremonial dress is paid for by the government.

The tunic is the most important—and expensive—single item. It is made from thirty-two-ounce wool ("scarlet beaver"), is hand-quilted, and has hand-sewn gold embroidery on the cuffs, slash, collar, shoulder straps, and back skirts. The cloth and the embroidery are made by old family firms in Soho, and the embroidery work alone takes about two months for each tunic. The finished article weighs about six pounds, has a life of three to four years if used constantly, and costs half the price of a small car.

Other items include the greatcoat ("Athol gray"), the blue trousers (twenty-one-ounce barathea), and the frock coat (thirty-two-ounce blue beaver), a rather dandy sartorial adornment normally worn by officers of field rank. One man, the Major General commanding the Household Division, has his entire uniform specially made for him,

103.

and one woman, the Queen commanding everybody, has her tunic specially made for her by Johns & Pegg but fitted and designed by her own tailor.

The reason the tunic is so heavy—it can double its weight with sweat on a hot day or with moisture on a rainy one—is that it must support the weight of the embroidery, which, being gold, is heavier than sin. It is also a tight fit. "That helps to keep the officer's neck up," said one of the military tailors.

The NCO's and Guardsmen make do with less elaborate uniforms. Their tunics, trousers, and greatcoats are machine-made. Imitation gold braid is used on their tunics, and their bearskins, coming as they do from the male instead of the female bear, are made of coarser and cheaper fur.

The Foot Guards, however, appear almost shoddy compared with the Household Cavalry. The cost to the government of the glittering glory of a cavalryman and his mount, be he officer or trooper, is the equivalent of a very expensive car. Whether all this is still necessary to "protect" the sovereign, maintain the standards of the Household Division and provide free entertainment for London's tourists is doubtful. But so far no one has seen fit to change it.

Windsor Castle: A Family Affair

It is a May day on the East Lawn of the Windsor Castle and the Queen is presenting new colors to the Irish Guards. The sky is overcast, but every now and then the sun bursts through, splashing light and warmth over the oaks, elms, and plane trees of Windsor Great Park, transforming it for an instant into a Turner painting.

The parade will take place on the grass, which has been given a close shave that morning and resembles a bowling green. The event is a family affair. Old comrades of all ranks greet each other and introduce their wives, relatives, and friends. The officers are dressed in morning coats and top hats and have mother-of-pearl pins in their ties. The NCO's favor navy-blue blazers with regimental badges on the breast pockets and wear Guards ties. The ladies are dressed, a little bravely, in summer frocks with hats and gloves.

A Labrador, led by a policeman, tugs at his leash and sniffs for bombs. There is an announcement on the loudspeaker: "Spectators are reminded that they are not to leave their seats until Her Majesty the Queen has left the East Lawn." In a corner of the grounds close to the castle walls there is a bronze statue of Queen Victoria's favorite dog, Dacho, sitting up on its hind legs and looking mournful.

There is a friendly, school-reunion atmosphere. The Irish Guards Catholic chaplain comes up to one of the officers and says, "Hullo, Mickey, how's your love life?" The officers, resplendent in their tunics and bearskins and sword belts, pose amid much bantering, under an archway for a group photograph.

The parade begins with the battalion marching up a daffodil-lined path under a canopy of venerable oaks to the lawn preceded by Cormach of Tara, the battalion's Irish wolfhound mascot. The Guards on the march have a special sway and swagger that marks them, but they no longer seem to be the giants they once were—a shortage of recruits has progressively reduced the minimum height to a lowly five foot eight inches. In addition to the regimental band there are the pipers, dressed in floppy Irish bonnets, green cloaks, rust-colored kilts, and silver-buckled shoes.

The new colors, hand-embroidered in crimson and gold, are pulled out of their sheath and laid reverently over a stack of drums in the center of the square. The clergy, who will bless them, add another dash of color with their magenta and purple cassocks. On the VIP stands there are rows of black and dove-gray silk top hats.

At one stage in the parade there is a strange piece of drill. "Battalion will remove headdress," comes the order. "Remove *headdress!*" This order leaves seven hundred men crouching with their rifles clutched between their knees, their bearskins off and held at shoulder height, and their close-cropped heads suddenly and shockingly naked.

After three cheers for the Queen, the skins of the male bear are returned to the heads of the Guardsmen and the Commanding Officer makes a "loyal" and somewhat excessive speech, larded with Your Majesty's this and Your Majesty's that.

The parade ends on an informal note. The Queen, dressed in a turquoise suit and hat that match the "St. Patrick's blue" plume of the regiment and carrying a black handbag, walks among groups of Guardsmen and their wives. The men duck their heads and the women curtsey as their Colonel-in-Chief stops for a brief chat and passes on to the next cluster. Her duty done, she disappears into the cavernous depths of the castle and everyone goes home, leaving Dacho in peace but looking as mournful as ever.

107.

The Queen inspects the Irish Guards at Windsor (pages 108–109)

Part III

Officers
and
Gentlemen

Making the Grade

*"I know from experience that in our army
the men like best to be officered by gentlemen, men whose
education has rendered them more kind in manners
than your coarse officer, sprung from obscure origin
and whose style is brutal and overbearing."*
Recollections of Rifleman Harris,
Peninsular War, 1808.

Q: "How does one becom
a Guards officer?"

A: (A Foot Guards major talking): "Well, anyone
acceptable for the Guards providing he is suitable with a big 'S.' W
look for common sense, manners, social graces, the ability to be at ea
in all circumstances. We don't need an extrovert personality. We wa
adaptability, and the NCO's want someone they can respect—tha
more important than ability because soldiers can be trained."

Q: "Suppose you had three candidates for one slot in tl
Guards. The first was brilliant but not from a public school and wi
neither family background nor money; the second was mediocre b
with strong family connections and a public-school education; the thi
had money, connections, and a public school behind him but w
rather stupid. Whom would you choose?"

A: "Let me answer that in my own way. Recently, we ha
an applicant with a working-class background who wanted to join u
He was first-class material, splendid officer potential, and he woul
I dare say, go far in the army. He would certainly be ruthlessly ef
cient. But the question I had to ask myself was—it was my job
interview him and make a decision about his future—*would he be hap,
with us?* I invited him home to supper to meet my wife and talk wi
her. I also talked to Guards NCO's who had trained him—they a
the best judges in these matters. What firm in civvy street would allo
its employees to comment on its future managers? Anyway, the you

man was terribly keen to join us, and we are, as it happens, desperate for officers. Yet . . ." the Major shrugged, "it simply wasn't right for him. It would have put him out of his depth—am I sounding snobbish? There is so much to consider. Would he feel at home in the mess, and what about his girlfriends, his eventual marriage, and so on? We have to be careful. There are no written qualifications for joining the Guards."

Q: "What happened to him?"

A: "He went to a line infantry regiment where he'll be an enormous success, I know it. And happy, too."

Q: "How did he react to his rejection?"

A: "Oh, complete and full understanding. Gratitude, too."

At Sandhurst a group of cadets, who will be shortly passing out and joining different Guards regiments, are talking and having their pictures taken. "The Guards make you feel wanted," says a young man who will be joining the Coldstream Guards after a brief period of leave. "At Sandhurst a lot of people don't hear from their regiments until the last week or so, and sometimes not even then. Whereas we get letters from our regiments throughout the course. If you do well at something a letter will arrive congratulating you. It's like a family. That's how they sell themselves."

And family connections usually help. "My father was in the Guards," says another cadet. "But he was quietly told he shouldn't have been there. He left after eighteen months. He doesn't object to me joining, but he says you must get out before you are twenty-six or twenty-seven, otherwise you become virtually unemployable."

A third says, "If I wanted to get a job, having been in the Guards, as an engineer in the Post Office then my chances would be slim. If, on the other hand, I wanted to be a stockbroker, then my chances would be high, do you see what I mean?"

"I joined for family reasons," says another cadet. "My dad was in the army, so was my grandfather and two of my uncles." A tall cadet, destined for the Scots Guards, says, "When I applied to join the Scots Guards, the Lieutenant Colonel commanding the regiment happened to be a very, very good friend of my parents and grandparents and his daughter was going out with my cousin. It was a bit of a farce as an interview—more like having a chat."

What if someone turns out to be a very good soldier, with a bit of cash in his pocket, but not of the "right" social background? "The way a senior Guards officer would answer that," says one of the group, "would be, 'We are not refusing that man because of his social status but simply because he wouldn't fit in with the other chaps in

The mess hall at Sandhurst (pages 114–115)

the mess.' That is so important in places like Northern Ireland and Germany. What do you think?"

He turns to his friends.

"The thing is," says another, "you can be a good officer, you can have money, you can know how to act, but you are still slightly out of it because you are joining an 'elite' group. Now I'll be able to walk into his mess"—he indicates his friend—"in two years time and know virtually everyone there from our age group not because we were at Sandhurst together but because I had met them at parties in London, or we had been to school together, or had met them at houses in the country, or perhaps our parents were friends. Do you see what I mean?"

The first cadet explains. "Everyone here has been to a public school. Now you don't *need* a private income any more, but it helps."

Is it possible then for someone who hasn't been to a public school to become an officer in the Guards?

"One man just tried and didn't succeed," says a cadet. "You see, basically you have to be happy in your regiment. He was a good soldier, but he wouldn't have been happy with us."

Does that mean that as long as the public-school system survives the Guards will survive?

"Yes, that's quite a good way of putting it. . . . The Guards are almost a public school in themselves."

Why not open up the officer ranks a bit more?

"Surely, if you opened up the floodgates you'd destroy the myth of the whole system. Guardsmen expect certain things of a Guards officer. They expect him to speak in a certain way, they expect certain aspects of manner, dress, and turnout, they expect him to go around doing strange things at strange times, to have a certain amount of style. Yesterday, during the middle of a rehearsal we came out onto the parade ground in a pantomime horse—I was in the arse—and everyone loved it. Of course they locked us up in the guardroom. Afterwards the Academy Sergeant Major said 'excellent.' England wouldn't be England without the Guards, would it? Guardsmen expect an officer to be a gentleman."

The Induction

Nine months after we talked to these young men, we caught up with one of them who had joined his regiment, the Scots Guards, in London. It used to be the norm that when a young ensign joined his regiment he was deliberately ostracized by the rest of the officers for the first few months.

"A friend of mine joined the Grenadiers," says this officer. "He went straight to Chelsea Barracks and a company commander sat down next to him at lunch and asked him how long he had been with the regiment. The chap said three weeks. Whereupon the company commander jumped up and said, 'Sorry, can't talk to you until you've been here for a month.'"

Times have changed, and now most newly joining officers seem to be given a much more friendly reception. Certainly, our man—we'll call him Michael—could not have been made to feel more at home. "There was no frostiness at all. Although I knew some people by name, I knew no one closely. I was fairly apprehensive, but they made me feel very welcome."

As he is talking, a boy who is "tasting" the Guards comes up and asks if he might try Michael's bearskin on. Apparently he has just left school, has been with the Scots Guards in Kenya on an exercise, and will probably be joining a Brigade Squad down in Pirbright soon.

"When I first joined the regiment," Michael continues, "I was spare. They put me in company headquarters as a glorified clerk, but then a couple of months later I was given a platoon and we went off on a very tough exercise in Scotland. I was lucky with my platoon because the former commander stayed on for two weeks while I understudied him, which was very good news." And the platoon sergeant? Silence for a moment, then a grin. "He is very competent, very capable . . . but I find him terribly overbearing. It's just that, well, I like to like the person I am working with.

"There is a difference between the Guards NCO's you meet at Sandhurst," Michael says, "and the NCO's you have in a regiment. At Sandhurst they know the sort of training you get, which is not much, whereas here the sergeants don't know that and expect more of you than you really know."

And the Guardsmen? "Terrific. About three-quarters of them are Scots, while the rest come from Preston, Carlisle, and the north of England. We are very proud of being Scottish—I am one hundred percent Scots—and nothing would please us more than to be based in Scotland. In fact, however, we are off to Belfast soon for a four-and-half-month tour.

"My job here, apart from the ceremonial, is to make sure my platoon's kit and barrack rooms are up to standard, train for Operation Trustee, which is protecting Heathrow Airport in an emergency, and looking after the Guardsmen's personal problems. For example, a Guardsman's father died the other day and luckily I was up in Scotland, so I went along and saw his family. Then you have things like a Guardsman getting some girl pregnant but she's married to someone else. It's incredible how complicated some of these things are. You're expected to solve the problem. But I enjoy that.

"I've done all the royal guards and other ceremonial parades," says Michael, who is sitting in the officers' mess at Chelsea Barracks dressed in his scarlet tunic. "Since I had only done my first color drill the morning before I went on guard for the first time, I was pretty worried as I turned the corner of Buckingham Palace and saw thousands and thousands of people. It was in the summer, and it's a long sweaty haul from here carrying the color. Actually, it's worse in a tunic than it is in a greatcoat because the greatcoat is looser-fitted and all you wear under it is a T-shirt."

How is the uniform issued to young officers joining their regiments? "In a very chaotic fashion," he says with a grin. "You charge around to all the different regimental stores. Of course, you don't pay for any of the ceremonial kit—unless you lose it. A sash alone will set you back five hundred pounds, but fortunately we all have pretty hefty insurance. We have to pay for our service dress, forage cap, Sam Browne, Blues, shoes, stars, beret, and so on, but you get a good clothing allowance. If you bought everything brand-new you would run over easily, but if you shop around carefully, get a bit of secondhand gear, some off friends, you might come out with a bit of a profit."

Is there financial pressure in the early days? "No, not really. . . . You have quite an initial outlay, but it's not too bad. Mess bills depend on the individual, but the average bill—messing, drinks, cigarettes, guests—comes to about half your net pay. I suppose I'm lucky because I get some help from my parents, and I couldn't really get by without that because I run a car, living in London is expensive, and I go home to Scotland quite regularly."

Another young ensign comes up, also in tunic order. "I woke up at ten-thirty and realized I was on picquet [guard]," he says. "Bit of a panic. . . . Is my forage cap in your room?" he asks Michael.

Before and after. Sandhurst to public duties. Sandhurst to Northern Ireland (opposite page)

When he has rushed off, looking rather less immaculate than the Guards officers the public is accustomed to seeing, Michael talks about his future.

"I'm looking forward to Northern Ireland, but I probably won't stay in the army after my three years are up. I loved Sandhurst and enjoyed the first few months here, but since then I've got a bit cynical. It's the tedium, I suppose. Though you are learning all the time. When it comes to learning about men, what actually happens in a platoon in barracks, you just don't know until you get here. It's really common sense, and you pick it up as you go along. I haven't the faintest idea what I am going to do after the army—agriculture perhaps, not university. You ask someone why they joined the army and you'll never get a straight answer because nobody ever knows."

How the System Works

The selection of Guards officers is not as casual nor even quite as elitist as one might think from listening to Guards officers talking about it. The best place to see how it is done is regimental headquarters. While the method of selection may vary a little from regiment to regiment, the basic process is the same for all the units in the Household Division.

There appear to be three main sources of supply. First, there are names put down at birth by keen parents or vigilant headquarters staff who monitor the birth columns of newspapers like the *Times* and the *Telegraph*; the names are entered on the "blue form" and filed in regimental archives. Then there are contacts made by military talent-spotters, former army officers who regularly visit schools around the country. Finally, there is the "walk-in" or spontaneous applicant. The most productive source, according to the Grenadiers, is the last category, with the liaison officers producing the next largest number of candidates, and the "down-at-birth" group being the least productive.

Those who have been inscribed at birth receive a letter from the regiment when they are fourteen or fifteen years old, and at sixteen they are interviewed. Visits to the regiment at the annual reunion and in the field are arranged during school holidays. A cadet at Sandhurst told us how impressed he had been when, as a "horrible scabby seventeen-year-old," he had been invited to "Grenadier Day" at Pirbright.

With everyone else off duty, The Duty and Picquet Officers of The Irish Guards dine in splendid isolation in the Officers' Mess at Victoria Barracks, Windsor.

"I was one of a group of about a dozen schoolboys," he said. "We were shown uniforms, helicopter and antitank demonstrations, the assault course, and given dinner in the mess. We were treated like officers throughout and made to feel throughly at home. Later, we were taken up to London to meet Prince Philip, the Colonel of the Grenadiers. I got the impression that the Guards were looking for the Eton type, but not the sort of person who had his nose in the air and did nothing."

The aim at the first interview, when the aspiring Guards officer is sixteen, is to sort out those who are considered suitable for the army from those who are not. The boy's headmaster is requested to submit a short report on his academic record and his general development. The second interview, at eighteen years of age, is more wide-ranging, although the first question the youth is asked remains traditional enough: Do you think you can lead thirty men in Northern Ireland into places they don't want to go? Another, more detailed report is supplied by his headmaster, as are character references from somebody such as a vicar, bank manager, or, preferably, an army officer who knows him well.

Height, still an important factor in the recruitment of Guardsmen, doesn't matter when it comes to the officers. One Guards officer who was only five foot two had no trouble getting in, but had to have a specially short sword made for him so it wouldn't trail on the ground.

According to officers in regimental headquarters in London, only very unsuitable candidates are filtered out at this stage. In other words, all but a few who apply or who are co-opted get into the mainstream of the army selection process, which, for the Guards, means the Brigade Squad at the depot in Pirbright, the Regular Commissions Board (RCB) tests, and finally, if all goes well, the military academy at Sandhurst.

"The regiment merely sponsors the candidate," said a member of the Grenadier Guards headquarters staff. "They are not actually accepted into the regiment until they have passed through the Brigade Squad and the RCB, and have completed three months at Sandhurst. This is our method of quality control."

However, since Pirbright relies entirely on the regimental headquarters for its supply of potential officers, those organizations clearly have a lot of influence in shaping the officer corps of the Guards.

What does the Lieutenant Colonel commanding a Guards regiment—he is actually a full colonel and a very experienced and

Lt. Colonel David Webb-Carter MC, Commanding Officer of the 1st Battalion Irish Guards, Victoria Barracks, Windsor (opposite page)

powerful gentleman—want in his future officers? "At the end of the day we are looking for three things," one colonel put it. "We are looking for men who can lead soldiers, whether it is training them, organizing sports, looking after their families, or taking them over the top. Secondly, we want someone who will be happy in the mess. And lastly, we hope to find people who have the capacity to develop and go far in the army as a whole."

And where do they find this material? "Since the end of National Service in the early sixties," said another senior officer, "the army has become more professional, more efficient, and we have broadened the field of recruitment for officers. However, the majority of our officers still come from the public schools, partly because more apply to us from those schools than any other, and partly because the public schools still develop the kind of qualities that the army needs in its officers.

"But," he continued, "we now take our people from a much broader range of public schools than we used to, and also from the top grammar schools. For example, the last group we sent down to join the Brigade Squad was an interesting mixture of the old and the new. Four from Eton, two from Harrow, one from Haileybury, one from Taunton College, and three from state schools—a grammar school, a comprehensive school, and a technical school."

The Regular Commissions Board, which determines who will become an officer in the British army, asserts that the most important distinction is not between public school and state school, but between boarding school and day school. However, since most public schools *are* boarding schools and most state schools are not, the net result is that the former maintain their advantage.

"Change will come," the Grenadier officer said, "when parents bring their children up to be more self-reliant and confident. This is what the public school does. The infantry may be a special case because it still requires a very young man of nineteen or so to lead thirty men into battle, some of whom will be much older and more experienced than he is."

The Guards, like other regiments, also commission officers from the ranks. The most traditional avenue is the promotion of senior warrant officers to the rank of captain or major as regimental quartermasters, a custom that dates back to the nineteenth century, when officers—like their gentlemanly counterparts in civilian life—shunned anything that smacked of "trade."

Each Guards battalion has an establishment of two quartermasters, with other quartermasters serving in extraregimental jobs.

There are, however, other promotions. These are short or regular service commissions granted to senior warrant officers who fill posts such as battalion military transport officer or are put in charge of welfare and the families. Their number is decided by the Major General commanding the Household Division, but it is usually not more than two per battalion.*

Although very experienced and usually earning more than their Sandhurst-trained counterparts—based on their long service as NCO's—these men are a distinct subgroup in the Guards officer corps. It is not that they are made to feel socially inferior—quite the reverse, for they are treated with great kindness and respect both at work and in the mess. Yet while they are not in purgatory, neither are they in heaven. They are in limbo. They will never be given a tactical command like a company or a battalion or a position of executive responsibility like an adjutant's job.

Their place in the pecking order, whatever their rank, is below the youngest ensign, fresh from Sandhurst. They will never wear the officers' soft bearskin; the not-undistinguished cocked hat is their ceremonial lot. In small but unmistakable ways they are repeatedly reminded of their station in military life. At the officers' mess in Pirbright, for example, the pigeonholes for the officers' mail are arranged in order of seniority, with the ex-rankers placed on the bottom row, after everyone else.

The staff list there underscores the social divide. Mainstream officers' wives have names like "Philippa," "Fiona," "Victoria," and "Serena," whereas the quartermasters wives listed are "Doreen," "Mary," "Pamela," and "Gladys." There are, however, compensations, and one the former NCO's value is the right to walk in and have a drink any time in a place where they once ruled supreme—the sergeants' mess.

A man who made this transition, after twenty years as a Guardsman and NCO, told us what happened and how it felt. "In the rest of the British army," he said, "when you get to the warrant officer level you can apply for a commission. In the Guards it's not like that. It's considered good manners to wait until you are asked. I was sent for by the regimental Lieutenant Colonel, a very nice gentleman, who asked me if I would accept a commission. It's a hell of a change, I can tell you. The best way I can put it is one minute you are the top man, as regimental Sergeant Major, and the next you're just another rabbit in the hutch. You go from God to being a mere mortal.

*Out of the Household Division's officer complement of 440, there are about 60 ex-rankers in these two categories.

"The officers in the regiment go out of their way to make you welcome in the mess. You know all the senior officers—you've probably been their company Sergeant Major at one time or another. All the same, you've got your place in the pecking order and you tend to stick together with the other quartermasters. . . . But let's be honest about it, the ultimate aim of every soldier is to be an officer. Now, the highest I could go is to a lieutenant colonel on the staff as a quartermaster, or if you are offered a regular commission—not on the quartermaster side—you still wouldn't command a rifle company or anything like that. And neither would you ever wear the officers' bearskin on parade.

"Is it upsetting?" he continued. "Not in the least. If you've got a touch of the Nelson about you, the cocked hat is very smart. Mind you, if you don't get used to turning corners sharply you can cut the head off of a lot of people. But I think it is time to let officers commissioned from the ranks do all the normal jobs in a battalion.

"The magic thing about all this is that you never leave your old comrades. You are always welcome in the sergeants' mess, and the unwritten rule is that you can go in there any time you feel like it. They don't feel you have abandoned them, and the fact that you have got commissioned is neither here nor there."

The Guards wouldn't be the Guards if there were no exceptions to the rules. Young men have begun their careers as Guardsmen, spent some time in that rank, passed RCB, gone to Sandhurst, and joined the mainstream of the officer corps. One notable case was a Grenadier who, in a very short time, became a lance-sergeant and drill instructor at the depot, went to Sandhurst, where he won the sword of honor, and later became adjutant of a Grenadier battalion. But such cases are rare.

Then there is a relatively new development that is causing the Guards some heart-searching. This is the rapid rise of a number of extremely bright NCO's who soon find their upward path blocked or slowed and decide to try for a commission. Some of them pass, go to Sandhurst, but are then transferred to an infantry or cavalry regiment of the line. They are not encouraged to return after Sandhurst to the Guards family.

The loss constitutes a small yet significant brain drain on the Guards. "Four of my platoon commanders are currently color sergeants," said one battalion commander in Germany. "Shortage of officers, you see. It was always said that it wouldn't work that way, but it does. They're bloody good. Those sergeants will eventually be commissioned, but the problem now is where will we get our grand old sergeant majors from in the future?"

126.

Officer of the Guard at Windsor Castle with telly (opposite page)
Early morning warm-up in Hyde Park. The Household Cavalry (pages 128–129)

Lifestyles

A great deal has been written about the Guards' style of living. The traditional image—so traditional that it has become a cliché—is one of effete opulence, of chinless wonders lisping their languid way through the moneyed upper reaches of society, as remote from the soldiers nominally under their command as they were from any other kind of reality. In short, rather similar to the dated Russian view read out to successive Brigade Squads at Pirbright and mentioned earlier in this book.

It is still an arresting fact that until a little over a hundred years ago, *all* commissions in the army were purchased and that officers needed no qualifications—and received virtually no training—for their job. The Duke of Wellington had pointed out earlier in the nineteenth-century that if you had gentlemen for officers you could not expect them to do many things, like speaking to the men. All that and much more was left in the competent hands of the NCO's. Thus it is only in the most recent third of the Guards' long existence that officers have come to be judged by the same standards as the men they lead.

However, the dilettante view persists. "The Guards and cavalry still perpetuate a lifestyle most people thought to have gone down with the Titanic," a journalist wrote in a British Sunday newspaper recently. And in Henry Stanhope's excellent book on the British army entitled *Soldiers*, a Guards officer stated that officers in the Household Division spent most of their time "chasing and killing things."

Although there is some truth in all this, it probably reveals more of how the Guards like to be seen—sometimes, clearly, with their tongues firmly in their cheeks—than it does of reality. Russell Braddon came nearer the mark in his perceptive and often very funny book on the Guards, *All the Queen's Men*, when he recounted the old joke—"You can always tell a Guards officer, but you can't tell him much"—and then went on to give his own judgment.

"The modern Guards officer," he wrote, "will probably not be an eccentric; he will certainly be a professional. He will be as elitist as ever; but he will not only look after his men, he will concern himself with the welfare of their families as well."

There is, of course, still a fair amount of high living in the Guards. But wealth, where it exists, is less ostentatious than it used to be and is more noticeable in the Household Cavalry than in the Foot Guards and more in the older Foot Guards regiments than in the

An officer of the Life Guards (opposite page)
The Household Cavalry under canvas in Surrey with guests and accessories (pages 132–133)

newer ones: the Grenadiers and the Coldstream seem to have more money around them than, say, the Irish or the Welsh Guards.

Guards NCO's, sharing the popular perception, will tell you that there is no way an officer can join the Household Division unless he has a substantial private income. The officers will laugh and tell you that that is what the NCO's—and the general public—love to think, but that it is simply no longer true. What does seem to be true is that while aspiring officers are told that a private income is not, repeat not, a prerequisite for joining the Guards, some extra cash would be extremely useful until they get on their feet in their regiment. They are told, for example, that it would be "nice" if they can afford a car when they are commissioned and the Navy, Army and Air Force Institute (NAAFI) can arrange favorable credit terms if necessary.

A senior Foot Guards officer put it like this. "When I first joined, you were expected to come with an allowance from your parents. That ended in the sixties. What I say to parents who ask me if their son needs an allowance today is, no, he doesn't. What he *does* need is somewhere he can get his head down when the bullets are flying overhead—letters from the bank manager, overdrafts, that sort of thing—so he can recuperate. And he does need help to get a car."

The more modest living is evident everywhere. Officer's cars are smaller, sometimes downright dowdy; bistro-style restaurants in London are now OK to be seen in entertaining wives or girlfriends; with the grand debutante dances defunct, young officers find themselves going to much smaller parties or slumming it in discos; small country weddings are replacing lavish military blowouts in London; officers are living *south* of the river, albeit comfortably, in hitherto unmentionable places like Battersea; and although food and drink flow in generous quantities in the mess as before and the same superb silver adorns the same gleaming mahogany tables, officers now serve themselves, cafeteria-style, at lunch and dinner.

Perhaps because the Guards officer corps is still such a club, the atmosphere inside it is very relaxed. Officers' messes are friendly, hospitable places and considerably more informal than those of many less famous regiments. In the Foot Guards only the commanding officer of the battalion is addressed as "Sir" by the other officers. When he is referred to in the third person he is simply called "Colonel John" or "Colonel Peter" or whatever his first name happens to be.

The degree of familiarity in Guards officers' messes would probably surprise people who think of the officers as stuffy martinets obsessed with rank and protocol. In one mess we visited, a young captain was being ribbed by his commanding officer about an ankle

A Household Cavalry farrier at work in Knightsbridge Barracks (opposite page)

injury that left him hobbling around in a plaster cast. The captain at first took it with good humor, but finally became exasperated and turned on his colonel and said, "With respect, sir, piss off!" The colonel and everyone else within earshot doubled up with laughter.

In the Household Cavalry, the commanding officer is addressed as "Colonel" by his officers. They show an additional measure of respect to him, the second-in-command, and the squadron leaders by clicking their heels at their first encounter of the day and saying, "Good morning, Jeremy," or "Good morning, David," as the case may be. This custom has been known to cause a small rift in Anglo-German relations when visiting German officers notice it and think the insouciant cavalrymen are poking fun at their Prussian past.

Guards officers traditionally give each other a piece of silver when they get married, but now the recipient has the option of suggesting something more practical or simply taking a check. One officer in the Grenadiers, who like many these days decided not to have a military wedding in London, which he said would have cost at least £10,000, chose a canteen of bone-handled cutlery instead of the traditional silver salver. "It's all very well if you have a butler to carry it," he said, "but no bloody good at all if you haven't."

In the Welsh Guards the customary gift is a solid silver Welsh dragon, which, when flame belches out of its mouth, turns out to be a cigar lighter. But again there are signs of the changing times. The dragon is now made out of silver plate. As a further economy, one officer pointed out delicately, indicating the beast's nether regions, the dragon is a gelding.

The Guards, a club in itself, is filled with other clubs. There are clubs for polo, sailing, riding, cricket, tennis, flying, shooting, fishing and many other activities. There is the Cavalry and Guards Club in Piccadilly, where Guards alumni can keep in touch with what is going on at the old school before they doze off, tactically concealed behind their copies of the *Times*. The Household Cavalry and the Foot Guards used to have separate clubs, but hard times forced an amalgamation in the sixties, which caused one crusty old Guards officer to splutter into his brandy, "We're not going to join the cavalry. They're shits, and besides, they smell."

Each regiment has its own clubs as well. The Grenadiers, for example, have the First or Grenadier Guards Club, which puts on an annual dinner for past and serving officers in the regiment. Then there is something a little more selective and secretive, the Blue Seal Club, which is in effect an elite within an elite. Membership is by invitation only and is confined to officers who have held command—adjutants,

A maker of gold accoutrements for the Household Cavalry (opposite page)

commanding officers, staff appointments, and so on—in the Household Division. But not all such officers are chosen. The club, which has about three-hundred members, meets once a year for dinner at the Dorchester Hotel in London. The Blue Seal Club is not a freemasonry, but it has masonic overtones. There is also a slightly schoolboyish air about it, with its office-holders rejoicing in such titles as Lord High Keeper of the Blue Seal and his Council of Tin composed of dignitaries like Chaffwax, Krousties, and the Keeper of the Purse. The club's motto is *Semper Vorax* ("Always Hungry"), and its address is simply Headquarters, Household Division, Horse Guards, London.

The Guards, like all military institutions, is an introverted, masculine world. The officers have wives, of course, but they are forgotten women. Though they occasionally appear on parades and at nonstag functions, they are, for the most part, safely tucked away at home. If someone wants to bring his wife or girlfriend into the mess for a drink he has to ask permission from his brother officers first. Many wives are themselves from military families, so presumably they know what to expect. From the fleeting acquaintance we made with them, we had the impression that although they were resigned to their lot, they were not very excited about it.

Then there is what might be termed the "peacock factor," the male warrior's delight in dressing up and, in the American phrase, "struttin' his stuff." The British army is renowned for the variety of its uniforms and for the idiosyncrasies of the men who wear them. Regiments and individuals stubbornly cling to pieces of apparel that signify a famous episode in regimental history, have an ethnic connotation, or simply express the personal taste of the wearer. Every attempt to create a unifying uniform on, say, the American model, has ended in failure, and the British continue to sport their exotic collection of berets, cap badges, tassels, lanyards, cockades, and other distinguishing plumage.

The Guards, being older than most, are more idiosyncratic than most. An American major, serving temporarily with the Blues and Royals in Detmold in West Germany, was amazed by the number of times the officers appeared to change their uniforms throughout the day. "Officers sometimes spend hours discussing what they are going to wear next day," a Grenadier confirmed in Berlin.

What Guards officers wore off duty used to be considered almost as important as what they wore on the barrack square. Pinstriped, conservatively cut suits, bowler hats, and rolled umbrellas—never to be unfurled, come rain or shine—used to be obligatory. But

A handful of London tailors have clothed the Guards officer corps for generations (opposite page)

now the rules are more relaxed, as they are with other things, such as officers being allowed to use London's public transport system and to carry parcels under their arms.

The officers of the Queen's Guard at St. James's Palace can swim or play squash at one of the Pall Mall clubs around the corner during their tour of duty. But in spite of more relaxed rules they must still walk there in full ceremonial uniform. And military decorum still insists that an officer thus attired may not carry anything else. So, at a discreet distance behind him, the officer's orderly will follow, bearing squash racket, shoes, shorts, jockstrap, swimming trunks, and anything else the officer may need.

The Flavor

Where things have not changed so much is in the flavor of the Guards officers' collective personality. Their image of themselves as professional—the best—yet relaxed, too, is unchanged. Similarly, they have retained the manic strain that has always seemed to be a part of them in peace and in war. To describe this with the written word is perhaps attempting mission impossible, because it is a subtle, intangible thing that can really be sampled only by spending some time in a Guards officers' mess, preferably late in the evening when the anarchic element is sufficiently lubricated and in a talkative mood.

Small things are an essential part of it. Dogs, for example. They are always around, whether it is the popular Labrador collapsed in a heap under the adjutant's desk, the wife's dachshund lost in a forest of brightly polished shoes and boots, a golden spaniel asleep against the bass drum that serves as a coffee table in the mess anteroom, or the pack of bloodhounds that the Blues and Royals hunt with in Germany and train in the tank park alongside their fifty-six-ton Chieftain battle tanks.

There is the flavor of the mess itself. There are military and royal portraits—the latter usually being rather awful and, though recognized as such by the Guards, irremovable because they were donated by former members of the regiment. There is the silver, often beautiful but not as plentiful or as lavish as that of many of the line cavalry and infantry regiments. The reason for this, apparently, is that the Guards never served in India, which seems to have been a rich source of "liberated" regimental treasure.

There are the uniformed mess waiters, the soft yellow light of the candles reflected in the polish of the dining-room table, the dog-eared edition of *Country Life, Field, Tatler, Illustrated London News,* and *Punch,* and innovations like the occasional copy of *Private Eye* and the television room, where someone might be watching "Top of the Pops" and be heard to comment, "It's about time we had a punk officer in the Guards."

Then there are the voices, the plummy accents parodied so devastatingly in Monty Python's "Upper-class Twit of the Year" skit and that foreigners so often mistakenly call "Oxford" English; it is, of course, public-school English. There are the jokes and teasing, the friendly banter with a schoolboy ring to it, which is not surprising since most of the men have gone from childhood to boyhood to manhood in identical enclosed environments. "We went to the same parties, the same races, the same schools," said a Coldstream officer. "Where else would I get a chance to work with the people I grew up with?"

The rich folklore of more extravagant days is preserved—and possibly improved—through repeated retelling. Mention the Life Guards and you will hear how they were alleged to have said, before the Second World War, "We'll dig the trenches and wait for the military to come." Someone is bound to recount the incident during the Suez landing in 1956 when a staff officer observed a three-ton truck stuck on the harbor ramp during the battle. "Who the hell are you?" he yelled. "I, sir," replied a dignified voice, "am the Mess Sergeant of Her Majesty's Life Guards, and I have with me the officers mess silver and champagne."

Bring up the First World War and you will hear about the young aristocrat in the Foot Guards who, returning from the horrors of the trenches in France, was asked by a London hostess what the war was like. "My dear, you'd never believe the noise," the officer replied, "and as for the *people!*"

Talk of the Grenadiers and you'll hear about the old general who, as Colonel of the regiment in the fifties, suddenly summoned all the officers to Wellington Barracks in London. They came from far and wide, thinking the Third World War was on the verge of breaking out. When they were gathered the general addressed them with a severe look on his face. "Gentlemen," he said, "it's come to m' notice that some of you fellahs are drinking a new-fangled thing called the cocktail. Gin and Indian quinine tonic water was good enough for me, and it'll be good enough for you. That's all. Good day."

Discuss the Irish Guards and the story of the sentry guarding an American missile site in Germany is told. A "full bird" U.S. colonel approaches. "It's OK, soldier," he says, "you can let me in." "No, it bloody isn't," replies the Guardsman. "No one is allowed to pass." "Let me in, boy," shouts the enraged colonel. "No one is allowed in. Stand back!" The colonel advances and receives a quick bayonet thrust through the loose skin at the side of his ribs. "And next time, it'll be through your middle," says the Irishman.

"We're in for the crack," say the wilder ones—funny, articulate, zany people who almost certainly will not last the course. These are the men who cheerfully purvey the more scurrilous anecdotes—about the cavalry officer who stuck up a bank with a shotgun that was worth more than the swag he stole, about the Life Guards being "a gaggle of professional wankers" (whatever that may mean), about the drum major who sold his color belt, and about the slogan of the Household Cavalry: "We may be no good, but we're stinking rich."

142.

A window in Clifford Street, London (opposite page)

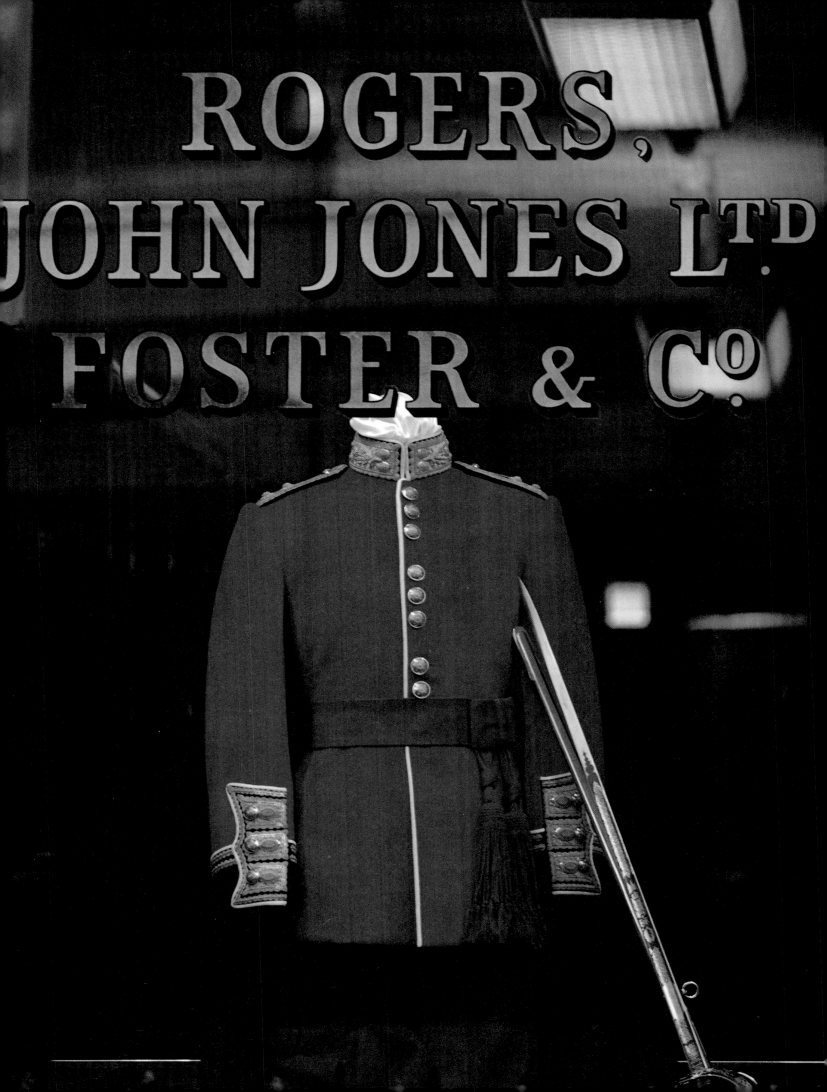

Part IV

The NCO's, The Other Elite

The Top Dog

"It is true that they [the NCO's] regularly get drunk by eight
in the evening and go to bed soon after.
But they always take care to do first whatever they are bid . . .
there is no one in the armies of the world
so intelligent and so valuable as an English sergeant
provided you get him sober, which is possible."
The Duke of Wellington

The striking Grenadier Guards Academy Sergeant Major at Sandhurst, mentioned earlier in the book, is a perfect photofit of what a sergeant major should be. He stands tall, even paradoxically when seated, his uniform is beautifully pressed—if ironing was an art-form his kit would be in the Louvre—he has a moustache, a rich, resonant voice with a trace of Lancashire in it, and possesses, in the words of a colleague and admirer, "more patter than a centipede with flipflops."

"Some time ago a very famous peer of the realm sent his son to the Regular Commissions Board," he says, "to see if he could pass and become an officer. When it was his turn to command the group of candidates in the obstacle test, he was told: 'Right, here's a river full of crocodiles. You've got to get your men across it taking this oil barrel and a couple of sandbags with you. And, by the way, this man here has a broken leg and has to go first. Carry on.' Well, the young chap lined up his group and, with three-hundred years of back-up in his brain, picked out the brightest-looking character and said: 'You're the platoon sergeant, carry on please.'"

The young aristocrat flunked the test and passed into oblivion, but he has remained a hero in the hearts of the NCO's of the British army.

The Academy Sergeant Major is in great demand as a speaker at schools, fetes and other functions. His oratorical talents have taken him to the United States where he has addressed American military organizations and has become friends with his opposite number, the senior sergeant major in the United States army. He plainly enjoys the showbiz side of the Guards and says, if Hollywood threw open the academy awards, the military would win every time. His great-grandfather fought in the Crimean War and his grandfather and father were also in the army although he is the first of his family to join the Guards. "In 1937 I was taken to London on a holiday and to this day I can remember the sentries at St. James's Palace. From that moment I just wanted to be a Guardsman. I left school at fourteen and when I was old enough I picked the Grenadiers because Manchester is a strong Grenadier recruiting area."

He believes that the links between officer, NCO and Guardsman in the Household Division are stronger than in any other military outfit in the world. "We have this magic, you see. But I wouldn't call the NCO's quality *power* as much as being able to handle both sides of the coin. The NCO's standing is the result of tradition. Guardsmen are a funny breed of people. They do not expect their officers to be the same as they are."

The telephone rings and he answers it in a crisp, assured tone. There is a Gurkha demonstration platoon at the Academy which shows the cadets how infantry tactics and weapon handling should be done. There is, apparently, no word for "academy" in Gurkhali and in their search for an approximation of his title the Gurkhas have come to call our man the "Atomic" Sergeant Major.

"In the Household Division an officer," he continues, "is an officer and a gentleman. End of story. If your ancestors weren't with us at Waterloo we're not interested. I'm a terrible snob, I'll admit that, a snob as far as the officer corps is concerned. No democracy there. What do I mean by an officer and a gentleman? My son-in-law is a captain in the Royal Engineers—my daughter did very well for herself, I think—but no way could I ever see him as an officer in my regiment."

"My son goes to military school and is oriented towards the army but I would never dream of having him in my regiment. Like all youngsters he doesn't want to start like Dad did but I would never direct him to the Household Division because it's not fair to him. He's not got the background. If he came to Sandhurst—he's now sixteen years old and I'll be here for another three years at least—it will be terribly difficult for him. He often says that the first thing he will do if he joins the army is to change his name. I would have to search my conscience very deeply to see if I would stay."

Outside the window a group of cadets pass by on bicycles

147.

and three joggers pound the turf alongside the lake that Napoleon's soldiers dug as they waited for the war to end.

"When I joined the army a hundred years ago," says the Academy Sergeant Major, "it was very hard. Physical violence was a way of life. If you did not throw that grenade correctly and get down in the proper way you got whacked over the steel helmet with an iron poker. That was the name of the game. All that has changed. The punishment system has completely changed. I think we threw a lot of good things out of the window but on reflection we are dealing with a completely different animal. More intelligent and better educated? Yes, I think so. No longer the blind obedience, if you understand what I mean. The days of fix your bayonet, charge that Russian tank—'right sir,' and away we go—those days are gone. Now the thing would be, 'excuse me, sir, are you sure you've got that thing quite right?'"

Not long after our talk, the "Atomic" Sergeant Major was offered an excellent job as administrator at Blenheim Palace, the Duke of Marlborough's stately home. He decided not to wait to see if his son would enter Sandhurst and left the army after thirty-five years of service. One of his former Grenadier comrades, on hearing the news, shook his head. "Pity," he said, "the likes of him are now as rare as rockinghouse turds."

The Other Elite

It is no accident that when an outsider watches the Guards at work the people he sees—and, of course, hears—are mostly NCO's. They are invariably big strapping men, immaculately turned out, utterly self-confident and they seem to be everywhere. In any army the warrant officers, sergeants, and corporals are an indispensable link in the chain that runs smoothly down from the commanders to the commanded, but in the Guards they appear to have a special position, an extra power and a particular aura.

The reason for that seems to be partly historical and partly the result of the control they exercise over the ceremonial aspect of the Guards' role. In the past during peacetime they did all the work anyway and although that is no longer true, Guards officers appear ready to delegate a wider measure of responsibility to their noncommissioned officers than is customary in the army as a whole. Then they are the acknowledged masters of drill and parade. The officers not only defer to that expertise but willingly submit to being trained, coached, and advised by their inferiors.

Unlike the officers, the NCO's have no formal training. There are no NCO academies, as there are in the American army, although there are specialized courses for those who are moving up the ladder. The raw material of an NCO is a Guardsman who comes up the hard way through the ranks, slipping every now and again perhaps when drink or some other temptation gets in the way.

Oddly enough, in an organization that prides itself on its discipline, being busted is not by any means an insuperable barrier to reaching the top of the tree in the Guards. "It's not as serious as it might seem," said a former sergeant major who had experienced the disciplinary roller coaster himself. "It even has some advantages because when you've been in the hole yourself no one else can tell you about it."

Guards NCO's have somewhat wider horizons than their counterparts in the rest of the army because of the Household Division's ceremonial function and the availability of prestigious jobs at Pirbright, Sandhurst, and other army teaching institutions. For example, at the Royal Electrical and Mechanical Engineers apprentice college at Arborfield and the School of Infantry at Warminster, the top NCO's are always Guardsmen. Even at the Guards depot there are extra-regimental opportunities in the All Arms Drill Wing which trains NCO's from other units—and from foreign armies—in drill and the art of the ceremonial parade. In a very real sense, the Guards NCO's are the British army's drill specialists.

But why such an emphasis on drill? "In the Household Division," said the Academy Sergeant Major at Sandhurst, "we think there is a correlation between drill, strict discipline, and military effectiveness. People say, 'God, you're finicky,' but when you're somewhere like Northern Ireland and you turn round and say, 'give me the spare battery for the radio we've got to go out on a quick patrol,' you don't want the guy to say, 'I've forgotten it, sir'. You want him to put the right kit in the right pouch and he will if on Day One you said that button is the wrong way up, those boots are not polished, your laces are twisted. We think the end product of all this is that it saves soldiers' lives."

The ceremonial is the NCO's very own show and they, for the most part, revel in it. Officers, as much as the Guardsmen, rely heavily on their inexhaustible supply of knowledge and skills. A common way of imparting some of that on parade is for the NCO to tell the officer under his breath what the next move is when he is saluting him. "Next order, sir," the color sergeant murmurs as the tourists watch unknowingly through the railings, "is *stand at ease*, sir."

151.

Drill instructors with pace sticks, Guards depot. Pirbright (pages 152–153)

There is a true story of a young officer, who feeling a little frayed from the previous night's social activities, was marching the Queen's Guard back from St. James's Palace. He was incorrectly carrying his sword at the *slope*—the blade resting on his shoulder—instead of at the *carry*—the sword carried vertically at right angles to his forearm. The color sergeant spotted the error and moved up slowly until he was alongside. "Carry your sword, sir," he muttered as the cameras clicked and the crowd cheered. No response. "Carry your sword, sir," he said again in a louder voice. Still not a flicker of response from the marching subaltern. "CARRY YOUR SWORD, SIR!" Contact at last. The officer painfully swivelled his bloodshot eyes. "That's quite all right, Color Sergeant. I can manage myself, thank you."

Discipline, in its broadest sense, continues to be one of the Guards NCO's principal preoccupations. Regimental sergeant majors exercise great power in setting the disciplinary tone of a unit as well as advising the commanding officer on the type and length of punishment for wrongdoers.

But, as the Academy Sergeant Major pointed out, times have changed. A Grenadier regimental sergeant major, one of the younger generation, put it this way. "There's no need these days to take someone around the back of the billet and beat hell out of him. I would be most annoyed if I thought any of my NCO's were doing that though, mind you, we have got one or two who could do with a good boot up the backside. You've got to motivate the men the right way and you'll get the best out of them."

Detention is still the worst form of punishment and up to twenty-eight days can be given at battalion level. Absence without leave for a longish period, say two to three weeks, would merit that kind of sentence. A man in detention is woken up at the crack of dawn, prepares his kit, is inspected, runs around with a pack on his back all day, is given all the menial fatigue duties around the barracks to do, has no privileges of any kind, and collapses exhausted at night. He will eat normal food—unless he commits another misdemeanour during that period in which case he goes on to bread and water—but at different times from the other soldiers.

The days of the lash are long gone but the older soldiers recall more violent times than the present. In the Welsh Guards sergeants mess in Bessbrook, South Armagh, the regimental sergeant major, shouting above the late-night singing of a well-oiled impromptu Welsh choir, described the difference.

"In the old days when I first joined, twenty years ago, the

154.

NCO's ran the place with this"—he pointed to a glass of whisky on the bar—"and with that"—he balled a fist. "Now it's different. Punishment is still there but it's milder—fatigue duty, extra drill, fines. The Guardsman is a much more intelligent, responsive and, I think, professional fellow today."

The military's passion for hierarchy is very pronounced among the Guards noncommissioned officers. A group of Irish Guards NCO's sat and talked about it in their mess tent in the humid, tropical warmth of Belize. "Our real boss," one of them said, "is not the commanding officer—he's just a figurehead, a man who deals with administration—but the guy who wears the ham and egg on his sleeve. [The royal coat of arms that designates a regimental sergeant major.] That's why we call him, 'Sir.'"

"We're also different from the rest of the army," said another, "in that we give our junior NCO's responsibility at an early age. A young lad will go straight from lance-corporal, who has two stripes because Queen Victoria didn't like seeing her guard mounted with a chap who only had one stripe on his arm, to a lance-sergeant. This means that he, as an equivalent of a full corporal anywhere else, will join the Sergeants Mess and get pulled up by his bootstraps pretty quickly. We also have much more responsibility than the line regiments. If you have to perform before five-thousand people with fifteen Guardsmen under your command you can't afford to blow your cool."

"There's no doubt that the regimental sergeant major runs the show," said a third. "By the time you've had twenty years of service, you should know what you are doing. You're responsible for discipline and administration in the whole battalion, and that's a pretty powerful job. And there's nothing wrong with the hierarchy. A soldier wants to know his place and in the army there is a place for everyone."

The Guards NCO's have more than a little in common with the craft guilds of medieval England. They are skilled but essentially uncreative workers who know that their livelihood depends on keeping the system as it is or, if that is impossible, ensuring that change takes place slowly and under their supervision. As a group they are the most conservative and most cohesive element in the Guards and their views seem to be sought and carefully weighed by the powers above them when change is in the air. "If you want to know what is going on in a regiment go the Sergeants Mess," is an old adage but it appears to have lost none of its wisdom in the modern Household Division.

In the Mess
Detmold,
West Germany

Detmold Barracks was built by Hitler for the Horse Artillery and is therefore not an inappropriate home for the Blues and Royals who in addition to their Chieftain tanks have twenty horses and a pack of bloodhounds with them. The mess, the social center of the NCO's life, is in a modern two story building, comfortably furnished, with a bar that would make many publicans green with envy over its design, stock, and, most of all, its custom.

The man who presides over this club is the Regimental Corporal Major—the cavalry equivalent of a regimental sergeant major—and is addressed as "Mister" by the officers and "Sir" by the rank and file. In the mess, as a concession to the social nature of the place, he is called "Governor," a custom that the more formal Foot Guards regard as an act of *lèse majesté*.

The Regimental Corporal Major has a carved wooden chair that looks a bit like a throne and is said to have been made by Hitler's carpenter. (The Hitlerian connection seems to have been strong in this neck of the woods.) "Only the Governor and the queen can sit on it," says another NCO with a grin.

The Regimental Corporal Major is a Scot, has been in the army for almost a quarter of a century and is, he admits, from the old school of noncommissioned officers. "I'm one of the last of that generation," he says in a strong Glaswegian accent. "Now, you can do what I did in fifteen years."

But he is only in his early forties and he does not want to leave the army. The trouble is that his regiment is only permitted to have seven officers from the ranks and all the vacancies are filled. "It's dead men's shoes now," he says with a smile, "waiting for someone to move on. Do I want a commission? Oh yes, it's the icing on the cake."

Over lunch which is served by mess orderlies and accompanied by a good bottle of hock, the Governor and some of the senior NCO's talk about their officers. The younger ones they treat paternally, the older ones with respect.

156.

Table setting, Blues and Royals, Detmold, West Germany (opposite page)
The Regimental Sergeant Major's batman cleaning his boots, 1st Battalion Grenadier Guards, Berlin (pages 158–159)
A mess corporal and a bit of the silver, 2nd Battalion Scots Guards, Chelsea Barracks (pages 160–161)

"We are encouraged by our officers to use our power," says the Corporal Major, "and we get a lot done at this level. We work very closely on a friendly basis with them but we all realize our positions and no one crosses that line."

"The young ones," says a squadron corporal major, "have to be taught. They haven't got a clue until they get to captain and sometimes if they do something wrong you have to bollock them."

The concept is interesting if a little unclear. How exactly, say, does a corporal of horse "bollock" a cornet? The men around the table laugh and look knowingly at each other.

"You take him to one side," says the NCO, "and you say, 'look, sir, you just made a horrible bleeding balls up. Don't ever do that again, sir.'"

But while the NCO's criticize the junior officers' competence they admire their spirit. They treasure a number of practical jokes played on newly-joining subalterns such as the one where a couple of young officers dressed up as NCO's. One of them pretended to be the Regimental Corporal Major who had been invited to dine at the officers' mess that evening. "I do like coming here," he confided to the bewildered newcomer as the soup was being served by a bogus mess corporal who, in turn, whispered in his ear, "can I be your orderly, sir? I do *like* you."

Another officer appeared in the anteroom rigged up as the padre and began drinking whisky (cold tea) by the half pint. "Bugger the Pope!" he yelled after a pint and a half. "Bring me another drink." The game finally came to an end when the cornet rang the bell for a drink himself and the orderly who had propositioned him fifteen minutes earlier came in and said, "go and get it your-bloody-self."

"Sometimes they kick up a hell of a row over there," says the Regimental Corporal Major. "One night they went a bit too far. So I walked over and told them to wrap it up. Ten minutes later the doors and windows were closed, the lights went out and all was peaceful once again."

Although not so raucous, the NCO's messes in the Household Division are very social places. The mess in Detmold is large with some 140 members compared with a mere 35 in the "other place." Mess balls and Christmas parties are elaborate affairs—the Grenadier Guards sergeants' mess in Berlin sat five hundred down to dinner not so long ago—and tend to outshine the officers' collective hospitality. The NCO's are invited over to the officers mess at Christmas and New Year's and many of them receive invitations to officers' weddings. The trend in sergeants' messes appears to be towards more entertaining,

A detail of the Drum Major of the Corps of Drums, 2nd Battalion Scots Guards (opposite page)

more formality—especially in terms of dress—and more funds flowing into the mess coffers.

Regimental sergeant and corporal majors have their own soldier-servants, called "batmen" in the Household Division while officers' servants are always referred to as "orderlies." Batmen and orderlies are regular soldiers but get paid a bit extra by their bosses and according to one sergeant major, "It's a good job for the lad who doesn't want to become a corporal and is good at kit." At large mess functions the NCO's dress up in mess kit as elaborate as the officers wear. In Germany, at least one regimental sergeant major was such a stickler for smartness that he refused to allow the Guardsmen to step out of the barracks in anything less than a collar and tie. "In the old days," a Grenadier officer said, "we always wore mess kit at regimental dances. It was the only way to stop the Guardsmen hitting you."

Like the Guards officers, the NCO's have their own clubs and societies outside the army. A notable one is the Royal Antediluvian Order of the Buffaloes, an organization that has similar masonic overtones to the officers' Blue Seal Club. Derby Day, at Ascot in June, is a popular spot for NCO's of the Household Division—past and present—and a special, well-victualled tent is erected to cater to this annual gathering of the clan.

The paternalism that is found in the relationship between Guards NCO's and their officers is frequently reversed when the time comes for a senior NCO to leave the army. It is then that the officer becomes the paternal figure using his contacts to get the man a new job or, in the case of the wealthier officers, giving him one himself. It often happens that an officer will be able to place his former company sergeant major or corporal of horse as the manager of his estate or find a niche somewhere for him in a company that he owns or has a interest in.

The more exalted the NCO the more elevated the job. A top NCO in the Household Cavalry left the army and got a job with the Duke of Roxborough on his extensive Scottish estate and a former Garrison Sergeant Major in London followed the path of many ex-servicemen into another kind of uniform, the white tie and tails of a doorkeeper in the House of Lords.

Chevron and sabre, Blues and Royals (opposite page)

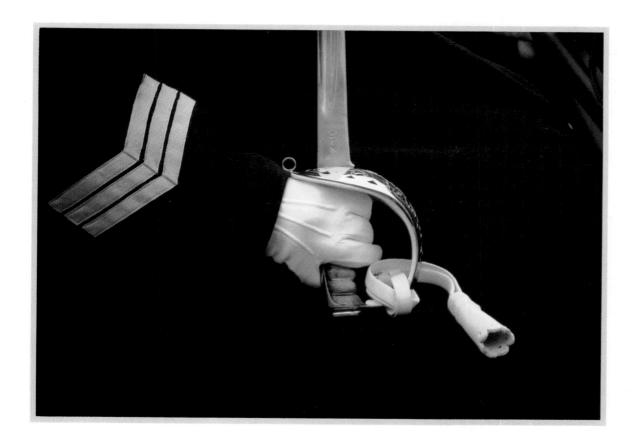

Part V

Crack Force or Colorful Anachronism?

Radfan, South Yemen

"Dogs, would you live for ever?"
Frederick the Great
addressing soldiers reluctant to advance.

Octover, 1967 We had set off shortly after sundown—four riflemen, a signaller, the sergeant, and I. Our mission, the company commander explained pointing to the map, was to make a large sweep around the camp and airfield following the rugged line of the hills. There was one risky sector, he said, a dried up *wadi* (streambed) where there was little cover apart from some boulders and clumps of camelthorn. The aim, the Irish Guards officer continued, was to flush out any Yemeni infiltrators who were running guns down to the terrorists in Aden and, in a discreet way, to show the flag. We would be back before dawn. "Carry on please, Sergeant."

We had been going for several hours. The sergeant told me to stick close and I stumbled along behind him. Before the moon had risen the dark had seemed the worst thing; now I wasn't so sure. We were climbing up a steep gulley, slipping and sliding on loose rock. The Guardsmen behind were cursing under their breath and we seemed to be making enough noise to alert every Yemeni dissident for miles around.

We reached the crest of the ridge and the sergeant raised his hand for a halt. The water out of the army issue bottle tasted metallic but cool. The moon, a slice of pale lemon hanging in the sky, illuminated the saw-toothed peaks and flung huge black shadows down into the crevices and along the twisting valleys. The camp was out of sight, hidden by a ridge, but we could see the end of the airstrip and directly below us was the sandy bed of the *wadi*.

Fifteen minutes later we were at its edge. The sergeant motioned the signaller to close up. The riflemen fanned out automatically in a covering arc behind us. We began to cross the *wadi*. I have no recollection of how far we had gone when the first burst of machine-gun fire raked the valley. I found myself flat on the ground, arms

168.

outstretched, clawing the coarse sand. Mortars, with their choking cough, joined the fray ranging ahead of us but getting nearer every minute. The temptation to leap up and run back to the safety of the hills was overwhelming. "Stay where you are," the sergeant hissed. He was a few feet away and partially obscured by a camelthorn bush. He yelled something to the signaller who had gone to ground several yards behind us. The radio crackled and the base operator's warbling Ulster accent came through loud and clear.

The shooting stopped. I raised my head cautiously but had no idea where it had come from. The sergeant pointed up to the crest we had just crossed and as he did so there were flashes and the thud of bullets striking the ground around us. The mortars opened up again, this time much closer. Another long burst of gunfire and the stock of the sergeant's rifle disintegrated. He groaned in pain. The signaller's voice rose above the din yelling the details of our position to base. "I'm OK," said the sergeant. "Keep your bloody head down." The machine-guns and mortars stopped and a stunned silence followed. I started to edge towards the sergeant. "Hold hard," he growled, "the chopper's coming."

The helicopter hovered and sand blew in our faces. A stretcher party jumped out and ran across the *wadi*. The company commander followed, his swagger stick in his hand. "All right, chaps," he said, "it's over." Over, I thought still on the ground, was it all some murderous kind of exercise?

It wasn't. The local sultan's forces, nominally allies of the British government, had got their lines crossed, and opened up thinking we were marauding Yemenis. At least, that was their story. "Silly bloody mistake," said the officer, apparently noticing the wounded sergeant for the first time. He walked over to him as the medics placed him gently on a stretcher. "Bad luck, sergeant," he said crisply and turned away to tell the ranking Guardsman to take over the patrol.

The Dual Role

The Guards, contrary to their stuffy, hidebound image, have been remarkably versatile throughout their long history. The Foot Guards, though infantry, have fought on board ships during the Dutch wars in the seventeenth-century, on camels in the Sudan, on horses during the Boer War—the famous "Aldeshot Mounted Foot"—and in tanks during the Second World War. Similarly, the Household Cavalry

has abandoned its natural habitat and gone to war on camels and bicycles, as artillerymen and machine-gunners and, in the First World War and Northern Ireland today, on their own flat feet.

At the beginning of the Second World War it looked as if the Guards would also fight on skis. A ski battalion, the "Snowballers," was formed under the command of a Coldstreamer to fight in Finland against the Russians. Many Guards officers chose to serve as Guardsmen and NCO's in order to be included, but the Finns capitulated the day the battalion embarked and that was the end of that.

The Guards have also shown a penchant for innovation that comes as a surprise to those who see them as sticklers for military convention. They have, for example, played a major role in the formation of the commando units, the Long Range Desert Group, and the Special Air Service (SAS). They quickly adopted airborne warfare tactics. Until 1975 there was an independent Guards Parachute Company and there is still a Guards group within the SAS known as "G Squadron."

Two members of that unit, a major and a sergeant from the Scots Guards, were sent to help rescue the passengers from a hijacked Lufthansa airliner in Somalia in 1977. They made their way to Mogadishu, the Somali capital, in civilian clothes posing as tourists and led the assault team of German commandos by blowing open the aircraft's doors.

Outside opinion of the Guards' military capabilities has nearly always been laudatory, from General Sir John Moore praising their discipline and morale in the retreat to Corunna at the beginning of the Peninsular War to Field Marshal Erwin Rommel commenting on their fighting qualities in the North African desert campaign. After the battle of Gazala, Rommel praised the Guards as being "almost a living embodiment of the virtues of the British soldier's tremendous courage and tenacity;" but he also said he thought they shared the faults of the British army too, notably "a rigid lack of mobility."

A more modern assessment comes from Field Marshal Lord Carver who said in an interview: "If you would ask me to defend a difficult position or attack in a set-piece battle, I would choose the Guards every time."

It is second nature for a Guardsman to switch from his highly visible ceremonial job to his far less obvious operational function and back again as the need arises, a unique doublehanded feat for any soldier. A Life Guard trooper is expected to sit his horse and drive his armored car with equal skill. A Blues and Royals trumpeter spends more time behind a 120 millimeter gun in a Chieftain tank than he does practicing taps. Guardsmen will be marching up and down outside St. James's Palace one day and patrolling the grimy, dangerous streets of Belfast the next. An officer in, say, the Grenadier Guards can make the transition from Windsor Castle to parachuting behind enemy lines as easily as he can change his socks.

The Household Division is not quite as homogenous as it looks principally because there is a functional difference between the Foot Guards on one hand and the Household Cavalry on the other. That distinction is largely the different roles that infantry and cavalry perform in warfare. The gap within the Division has been narrowed since the Household Cavalry began sending its recruits for basic training at the Guards depot in 1969. Nevertheless, pride of regiment and pride of role are powerful forces and if you ask a Life Guard or a Blue and Royal what comes first, being a Household Cavalryman or a member of the Guards he will invariably say that he is a cavalryman before everything else.

There is a pungent, albeit friendly, rivalry between Guards regiments. The Grenadiers are said by their rivals to be thick, pompous, and voracious eaters of Mars bars . . . the Coldstream Guards are described as being very laid-back and are thought to make excessive use of G. F. Trumpers' bathroom unguents (unreliable sources report that "Ajaccio Violet" is a favorite) . . . the Scots are alleged to be cold and humorless, and their officers not Scottish at all (they are often referred to as the "Surrey Highlanders") . . . the Irish have a reputation for being the opposite—warm, lovable, and funny too . . . the Welsh are universally regarded as being very nice and may have other sterling qualities which are unfortunately obscured because no one can understand what they are saying . . . and the Household Cavalry are reported to be effete, of dubious sexuality, and dripping with money.

Tanks and Guns, Horses and Hounds

Detmold, West Germany. Detmold, an attractive country town with a long military association, is situated on the north German plain, an area of sandy pine woods excellent for tanks but not so good for the hunt. The barracks were built in the thirties, solid, unexciting fascist architecture though adequate for the needs of the Blues and Royals who alternate here every four years with the Life Guards.

The other duties of The Life Guards, Windsor Castle (pages 174–175)
Dealing a hand in the Guard Room, Windsor Castle (pages 176–177)

The regiment is armed with the Chieftain tank, the main battle tank of the British army, and forms part of the NATO "shield," the theory being that if the Russians started to roll westward during the next Armageddon the Blues and Royals, along with other units of the British Army of the Rhine, would roll them back again.

"The Chieftain is a great bloody tank to go to war in," says an NCO slapping its gun barrel, "because it will break down before it gets there."

The tank park, not the parade ground, is the gritty center of life in Detmold and working on the beasts, cleaning, maintaining, and repairing them, and going on exercises in them occupies the major part of the regiment's existence.

The tank weighs fifty-six tons, is armed with three machine-guns in addition to its main gun, has a crew of four, and can, when the engine is having a good day, bowl along at thirty-five miles-per-hour. The troopers tend to agree with the army's claim that it is the best defensive tank in the world which, says a crewman, is "fine because we ain't going to Moscow."

The Chieftain is heavily armored and its 120 millimeter gun packs a more powerful punch than any other comparable tank. It is surprisingly easy to drive, rather like piloting a huge armor-plated motor-bike with kick gears and two levers to steer with. The main problem lies with its engine which is underpowered for such a heavy machine and prone to frequent breakdowns.

"British Leyland rubbish," comments a driver climbing out of his seat in a Chieftain that has broken down on the pine-forested training ground just outside Detmold. He disappears in a cloud of dust raised by two German Leopard tanks—small, immaculate, and fast—that roar past disdainfully.

The Blues and Royals, like the rest of the army, are short of equipment, spares, and ammunition. Training is severely limited by budgetary considerations and the best military hardware seems to be sold abroad rather than given to the army. The most sophisticated Chieftains—the Shir—were being sold to the Shah of Iran before his government fell. His demise has meant that armored regiments are now slowly getting the Shir tanks. In any event, the Chieftain is an expensive item, costing close to half a million pounds per tank. "It's not a good idea to lose one," says the adjutant.

The first sound that frequently reaches the regiment's ears in the morning is not the bugle calling reveille but the primitive bray of the huntsman's horn. At the end of the officers' mess there is a sign that reads: "Stables, Blues and Royals," an establishment that accommodates twenty horses; and then down near the tank park are the kennels, home of eighteen energetic and odiferous bloodhounds.

The pack is supported privately by the Blues and Royals hunt though the horses belong to, and are maintained by, the army. The master of hounds is a captain whose room, according to a less horsey officer, "stinks like a ferret's cave." But the hunt is popular with officers and troopers alike and seems to have none of the social pretensions associated with its counterparts in England.

The bloodhounds—rarely used as hunting dogs these days— each polish off four pounds of meat a day and rejoice in names like Kojak, Actress, Casper, Adjutant and Harlot. Their quarry when they go out is not a stag, fox, or hare, but a man running for his life dragging an aniseed-impregnated sock. Most days, however, they will be taken out around the tank park where an early morning visitor will see them being trained and exercised by the master on a strapping hunter and his "whipper in" dressed in a T-shirt with crossed foxes on it, a pair of army trousers, a trilby and mounted on a bicycle.

Detmold Notebook

General feeling, very relaxed. Virtually no drill except an early morning parade. Little "bulling"—the tanks are the thing. Discipline seems excellent though understated. Soldiers on the average seem brighter and better educated than the Foot Guards. Have to be to cope with the complexities and foibles of the Chieftain tank. Also seems to be a difference between those who serve in the Mounted Regiment in Knightsbridge, drawn equally from the Blues and Royals and the Life Guards, and the lads here. "Thickies ride the horses," says someone, "while the bright boys ride the tanks."

Officers' mess is a cavernous place, big enough for a brigade if you stacked them vertically. Formal dress-black tie for dinner—informal behavior. Young officers are not ignored in the mess as happens in some of the Foot Guard regiments. "Frightfully pompous habit," says a subaltern. But cavalry custom of clicking heels to field officers first thing in the morning takes a bit of getting used to; as does the alcoholic capacity of some of the wilder spirits who buck tradition by wearing frilly shirts under their dinner jackets.

High jinks in the mess, as described earlier, can lead to heavy bills at the end of the month but there is more money around than in the Foot Guards. Roughly a third of the officers are said to have private means. Same proportion—but not necessarily the same group—have university degrees, the army average. Lots of double-barreled names but wait till you get to the Grenadier Guards, they say, they're full of triple-barreled handles.

Loads of history around as one might expect when two seventeenth-century cavalry regiments amalgamate and pool their folklore. Portrait of a bonny eighteenth-century colonel, aged twenty-three. He had been, the record says, a major at the mature age of eleven. Black felt under the Blues and Royals cap badges commemorates the battle of Dettingen in 1743 when the Royal Dragoons—the "Royals" partner in the present regiment—whipped France's "Black Musketeers."

Kaiser Bill's picture also hangs in the mess. He was colonel of the Royals for twenty years, an appointment that came to an abrupt end with the outbreak of the 1914–18 war. He retained fond memories of his regiment and after his abdication sent them a Christmas card every year.

Reading material in the mess: *Horse and Hound, Country Life, Shooting Times, Punch, Tatler, The Field, The Countryman* and, for the highbrows, *The Economist*. Great variety of hats, canes, and crops spotted in the cloakroom; silver backed hairbrushes, combs, mirrors, and so on in the gents' lavatory; and lovely, highly polished brown shoes everywhere. Groups of five or six officers share the labor of a single orderly and pay him out of their own pockets. Only the commanding officer has his own full-time soldier-servant.

The old nanny network: a young captain reveals he shared a nanny at a tender age with a Foot Guards contemporary whom we had met at Pirbright. The world may be getting smaller but the Guards' world is still the smallest. Although the Household Cavalry poke fun at the Foot Guards—"wooden tops" and such names—they admit that if it came to a war they would feel safest with the Guards or the Scottish regiments beside them.

When the Blues and Royals leave Germany they swap over with the Life Guards in Windsor and take over their Scorpion tanks, a lightly armored reconnaissance vehicle armed with a small gun. They leave their Chieftains, horse, and hounds behind them. Like the Life Guards, they also supply men to the ceremonial unit, the Mounted Regiment in London, and what with periodic tours as infantry in Northern Ireland, they are feeling the symptoms of the British army's endemic disease, "overstretch."

All of which may have led to an Australian officer making the following comment about the officers in the Household Cavalry. "They're like a duck, all smooth and lovely on top," he said, "but underneath they're peddling like fuck."

A Blues and Royals Chieftain tank during maneuvers in West Germany (opposite page)

A View from the
U.S. Cavalry

Tucked away in the tightly sealed monogrammed casket of the Household Cavalry is an old gem, an American major commanding a squadron of the Blues and Royals in Detmold. A seasoned veteran who served in the air cavalry in Vietnam flying Cobras and other helicopters, he is spending two years on an exchange program as a fully integrated officer in the regiment. Two things have made an impact on him from the day he arrived, one favorable, the other less so.

The first is the power of the NCO's. "It's something that's really a shame we don't have in the U.S. army," he says. "When a young corporal tells a soldier to do something here he responds immediately without hesitation, whereas we have to spend a lot of time explaining why."

The second observation concerns uniforms. "In the U.S. army we have a uniform we wear every day. It is a functional duty uniform and even our generals wear it all the time. So, if we go down to the tank park and get dirty, it's no big thing. We don't change uniforms three or four times a day like the chaps here. I find that very distracting for the daily routine."

The major sits in his squadron office in his "functional" drab green uniform, name-tag stitched over his breast pocket, and attended by his British squadron corporal major, his squadron clerk and the rest of his staff. In a little less than two months he seems to have settled in quickly and comfortably and to have already picked up some Anglicisms like "chaps."

Yes, he's heard the comment about the officers in the Household Cavalry being laid-back but he hasn't seen it. "They're very professional in a calm sort of way. They don't yell and scream at each other and get excited," he says. "They do have certain social things, polo and what-have-you, but when they're supposed to do something they do it very professionally."

Since he's fought in a war, how does he think the Blues and Royals would react in "a combat situation?"

"I think they would handle it very well and I say that simply because of the discipline that I see throughout the regiment. Let me define that. Discipline in a unit means to me two things. First, a willing

182.

obedience to orders—when they're told to do something they do it. The second thing is something I consider to be the most important aspect of a disciplined unit and that is action in the *absence* of orders. When the leader isn't there do the soldiers play around or do they do the job?

"Well, when I go down to the tank park here I see that action, even without the NCO's. I see troopers there doing things on their own initiative. That tells me should the tank commander be killed in battle, or the officer—the troop leader—or the Noncoms get killed, those soldiers know their job and they will go out there and respond and, if it is required, fight to the last man. What motivates them? Probably their own personal pride and pride in regiment—we're the best—that sort of thing. I also think they get job satisfaction, they get some enjoyment out of what they are doing. They impress me."

Guarding the Frontier against the Guats

Few people seem to be aware that British redcoats are still on active service on the American continent. Yet they have been in Belize, formerly British Honduras and still a British colony, for some time now. They arrived as the result of belligerent threats made by Guatemala which claims its small, English-speaking neighbor as its own territory.

The most critical sector is the south-western corner of Belize, a mountainous jungle-clad region that forms the border with Guatemala. The trouble began in the early 1970's when the Guatemalans moved armor and troops up the dusty frontier road in an assertion of their "historic" claim. At the request of the Belize government, Britain responded by flying in troops. They have been there ever since, patrolling, conducting maneuvers, strengthening the border defences, flying their Harrier "jump" jets in mock strafing runs, and generally showing the flag.

The soldiers sent to protect Belize reflect Britian's ethnic diversity and its imperial past. The Irish Guards are in the southern zone, having taken over from the Gurkhas a few months earlier, while the Black Watch look after the northern part of the country. The local population, a pot-pourri of black Carib, African, Indian, and mestizo stock, welcome the soldiers and make them feel at home.

The nerve center of the Irish Guards operation in the south is "OP Cadenas," a tiny hilltop observation post perched five-hundred feet above the river-frontier. The only practicable way in is by helicopter and the journey takes about half an hour from the battalion's main base at Punta Gorda on the coast.

The flight is over an unending carpet of green with occasional clearings where Maya Indians have burnt the dense foliage. The terrain becomes more rugged and rolling in the interior and the pilot follows a pea-green river that has suddenly appeared, twisting and looping through jungle that would take days to cover on foot.

He switches on his radio and tells OP Cadenas he is coming in. An unintelligible Belfast burble says, presumably, that's fine. The aircraft tilts its nose and there is a change of tone in the fluttering thump of the rotors. A last gentle swoop and we are hovering directly over the OP. Looking down there is a bird's eye view of the ground below, an aerial picture framed in the mind.

The first thing to be seen—and, of course, it is intentional—is the Union Jack waving from its pole. The OP itself is built of stone on the flattened top of a high ridge, a meager space of about thirty feet by sixty feet where ten soldiers live, watch, and if necessary, fight. The ground drops away precipitously on all sides of the ridge but provides a perfect panorama of the valley below. Across the river there is a major truck road, a border post, and a Guatemalan military camp called Puerto Mendez.

The chopper circles, the pilot timing his descent on the pocket-handerchief landing zone with care. Two Irish Guardsmen, stripped to the waist, crouch near the landing zone with batteries and other stores going back to base. A slight bump as the landing gear grates on the limestone filling. The doors are opened and we are out running, heads tucked in, stumbling on the stone chips, the small hurricane from the rotor blades lashing at hair and clothes, sending dust and fragments flying—for a moment the Hollywood military fantasy of your choice.

The man in charge of OP Cadenas is a sergeant, six-foot six-inches of well-honed sinew and muscle, eighteen years in Her Majesty's Foot Guards, former army heavyweight boxing champion and British Empire silver medallist. An ideal chap, in the opinion of his military superiors, to defend the imperial frontier against the "Guats"—the universal term for Guatemalans among British soldiers.

184.

Sergeant McKinty, Irish Guards, keeping an eye on the Guatemalans (opposite page)
The Pipes and Drums of the Irish Guards in their Belize base camp (pages 186–187)

The sergeant has nine men with him, while down in the valley in Puerto Mendez there is a force of 4 officers, 9 NCO's and 124 soldiers. In the gloom of the observation post there are three essential pieces of equipment: a telescope, a radio, and a machine gun. Two Guardsmen are seated behind the telescope, one watching and reporting what he sees, the other writing down every detail in a logbook in front of him.

"Soldier—an officer—coming out of the bakery. Armed, with a pistol. Walks across road, goes into quartermaster's store." There is a scratch of a pen as the soldier-scribe writes, noting down the time of the event. The radio crackles. It is the Irish Guards' base camp calling, a routine check. Back at base an officer put it this way: "There's not much that misses us down at Puerto Mendez. We even know when the commanding officer is getting his leg over."

That vigilance is maintained around the clock. There are always two men on duty and the radio link remains open all the time. When darkness falls the telescope is removed from its stand and "Noddy" set up in its place. Noddy is the acronym for "Night Observation Device," a high-powered, infra-red telescope that gives the lonely watchers on the hilltop perfect night vision.

The sergeant sits beside the machine-gun. "It's aligned on a number of fixed targets," he says in his Ulster brogue. "The orderly room, the fuel and ammunition dumps, the officers' quarters, and so on. That means we can keep up rapid and sustained fire at any time of the day and night and be sure that we are hitting something that matters."

The need has not yet arisen. All is quiet on the Guatemalan front but the British army, having been unpleasantly surprised on this side of the Atlantic before, is not taking any chances. The last bout of Guatemalan aggressiveness coincided with presidential elections when a favorite song began "Belize is Guatemalan" and the armor came rumbling up the road.

Over the last few weeks, there has been some activity down at Puerto Mendez as Guatemalan army engineers build a new road. But there is no sign of belligerent intent though the situation is expected to warm up at the next presidential elections for, despite protracted negotiations, Guatemala's claim to Belize has not yet been amicably resolved.

What would happen if the Guats *did* attack? "If it was just a few rounds," the sergeant says, "we'd lie low and hang on. If it got heavy it would be up to the army command back at base or in Belize City to decide what to do. If it got really rough we'd probably bail out and cover our exit with this." He taps the machine-gun in a most friendly way.

"Bailing out" is not as easy as it sounds. There is only one walkable track down from the hilltop but it goes in the wrong direction, that is, down to the river border. The route the Guardsmen would be compelled to take is more complicated, especially if the evacuation had to be done at night. Behind the observation bunker and facing in the opposite direction are the mens' sleeping quarters. Below them are two stout ropes tied firmly around a rock and running down off the hill, almost vertically, into the dark green abyss of jungle below. This is the escape route.

Once the order to abandon the OP is given everything that could not be taken with them would be destroyed and the flag would be hauled down for the last time. The sergeant and his men would load as much as they could carry on their backs and slide down the ropes to the valley floor. They would then face a forced march through the jungle, following a prepared trail marked by splashes of white paint on the trees, to another better protected landing zone where helicopters could fly in and lift them out.

The tropical night is closing in and our helicopter pilot is eager to get away. The Guardsmen have just finished their evening meal and a couple of them are sitting around drinking beer. They clearly like and respect the sergeant enormously and say they prefer it out here in the jungle to marching up and down in bearskins and scarlet tunics outside Buckingham Palace.

Despite the long and bitter struggle in Northern Ireland there is no animosity between Catholics and Protestants or northerners and southerners in the Irish Guards, although the regiment continues to maintain its "ethnic" traditions by recruiting from Ireland and Irish districts in Liverpool, Manchester and London. Of course, in common with the other Irish regiments in the army, the Irish Guards do not serve in troubled Ulster.

"Sure, it all comes out a bit when the lads have had a few pints," says a corporal. "The Protestants sing 'The Sash My Father Wore' and the Catholics belt out the rebel songs. But it doesn't go any further than that."

"Isn't that right, Paddy?" he says to a Guardsman, an old soldier who is drinking beer from a can.

"If you say so, Corporal. A few of me family were in the IRA, you know."

"Then why did you join the Micks?"

"The Guinness is cheaper."

The last post. Piper Strannock, Irish Guards (pages 190–191)

The sergeant has invented a shower, a strange contraption of pipes, tanks, and hoses that works from rainwater sluicing down the roof of the billet and the waste running off the hillside. Before he installed it the only way the men bathed during their week-long stint at OP Cadenas was to stand out in the open when it rained with a bar of soap in their hands. "The trouble now," he says with a grin, "is that since I finished it three days ago there hasn't been a single drop of bloody rain."

There is the *whump-thwack, whump-thwack* of the helicopter's rotors beginning to turn. The sergeant picks up the book he has been reading—Spencer Chapman's *The Jungle is Neutral*, a seminal account of warfare in the Malayan jungle in the fifties—and waves goodbye with a hand that would have no trouble felling an ox. The "Micks," still stripped to the waist and apparently oblivious to the man-eating mosquitoes, give the thumbs up sign.

A touch of Kipling, a trace of *M★A★S★H* but serious too. Britannia's last imperial outpost in the Americas is secure for the night.

The Problem Areas

A middle-class Englishwoman, on being told about this book when it was in preparation, made a not untypical comment: "What's there to write about?" she asked with a laugh. "They're all queer and too thick to do anything else. To get in, your father had to be one of them anyway."

A senior Guards officer said during an interview: "There are three boring things—elitism of the officers, black men in the Guards, and homosexuality—and you've hit on all three. I'm actually very bored with all of them."

Well, boring or not, these topics do come up time and again in the public view of the Guards and within the Household Division itself. For, hermetically enclosed though they often appear to be, the Guards nevertheless keep a cautious eye out for what is happening

Fortified helicopter pad, Bessbrook, Northern Ireland

around them. And although they are confident that they have got things just about right they are neither smug about it nor impervious to criticism.

"Elitism? What's wrong with it? It works!" In the past, the army in Britain was a recognized way of translating wealth into status. Up until 1871 all commissions were bought, the more exclusive the regiment the higher the price. Today, the army as a whole serves no such function. However, certain regiments like the Foot Guards and the Royal Green Jackets in the infantry and the Household Cavalry and the famous Lancer, Hussar and Dragoon regiments in the cavalry still confer social prestige on their members and, more important, continue to open doors along the corridors of power.

There are, of course, other elites, the tough or "macho" units, such as the Parachute Regiment, the Special Air Service, and so on, but their prestige is exclusively military.

"The only excuse for this elitism," said a Foot Guards major, "is that it works. It works in a military sense and very efficiently because we have all been educated together, we all have the same assumptions and interests, and we all know we will work together as a team. All the people with whom one has most in common tend to be in the Guards—putting it bluntly, people of the same class.

"We are out of step with the rest of the army in the sense that we maintain a degree of social elitism," he continued. "But I don't think there is any need to make excuses for it. In Britain as a whole the elites have changed and I would say our intake of officers has changed in line with that development. There are far fewer high-born people in the Guards today and money is much less important than it used to be. And if you look at a group of merchant bankers, the City of London, the Foreign Office, or at the top of any profession—look at the cabinet with all its Old Etonians—you'll see that the Guards are not unique in this sort of power relationship."

The fact that the Guards' brand of elitism begins in a family environment and is reinforced in the preparatory and, later, the public school crèche means that Guards officers are rarely exposed to anything else. Russell Braddon, in his book *All the Queens Men*, drew the following conclusion.

"Pirbright, Sandhurst, the regiment to which he [the officer] proceeds on passing out, and the army itself will all perpetuate the public school pattern. At school the potential Guards officer will have advanced from nonentity to exalted sixth former. At Pirbright he will revert to being a nonentity, but go from it to Sandhurst with a sixth former's sense of predestined glory. Only to be treated like dirt at Sandhurst until, a sixth former again, he passes out and enters his regiment—as a mere nothing—in the hope that some fifteen years later he might become its head boy. As which, at the bottom of the hierarchy of field officers, he will be almost a nonentity again."

A development that has stretched the Guards officers' horizons a little is the number of university graduates that are now coming into the army. Roughly a third of the officer corps has been to university and while some military purists contend it is not necessarily a good thing, mainly because graduate officers miss valuable on-the-job experience and their rapid promotion without it can cause resentment, the army hierarchy is keen to attract as many graduates as it can.

"The aim is for all officers to be graduates," said a battalion commander, "but it is difficult to get the mix right. A graduate will spend a year at Sandhurst and then three or four at university and may therefore never command a platoon since he will join his regiment as a captain. The NCO's call these men 'educated idiots' which is not fair. But it's a fact of life in the infantry that you must have platoon experience to be a good officer and you can't get experience commanding people at university."

"My view is that the graduates are sufficiently bright to make up for lost time and catch up," said another officer, himself a graduate. "It may take two or three years but the end result is the same. The NCO's are notoriously conservative and the university idea does not conform with their pattern of how things should be done. You know, the sort of thing that so-and-so is not a proper officer because he hasn't been under a sergeant's wing for two years. In fact, it is often to an officer's benefit that he hasn't because he also learns bad habits there. The other thing is that university training makes people more interesting, it gives them a measure of adaptability and makes them more complete human beings."

"It's something I've never worried much about," commented another battalion commander. "What the army wants to do is get its fair share of graduates. I find some are better and some worse than the non-graduate officers. Some regiments have two distinct camps: graduates and non-graduates. Well, I've never known that to happen in the Household Division.

"There is a disadvantage about being a graduate officer in that by the time you have arrived people who are younger than you will have actually had more experience in commanding soldiers. That is a problem, but I wouldn't exaggerate it."

Graduates are not spread evenly throughout the Household Division though the overall figure corresponds approximately to the army average. When it was pointed out to an Irish Guards officer that his regiment was well above the average—fifty percent were graduates in fact—while the First Battalion, Grenadier Guards, could only muster two university degrees in the whole battalion, he smiled and said: "That speaks for itself, doesn't it?"

The ability of the Guards to maintain their elitism has attracted people who are fleeing, as it were, from the inroads that social democracy has made on other formerly exclusive preserves. We came across several young men whose families had, for example, traditionally served in the Royal Navy. "The Navy has become so *dreadfully* cosmopolitan," said a Scots Guards subaltern in a shocked tone, "that there was no question I would go into it."

There is another kind of refuge that the Guards provide and that is a measure of relief from the intensely competitive animal that the modern army has become. That is not to say Guards officers lack drive or ambition—far from it. They have more than their fair share of top jobs in the army, gained if anything against an inverted prejudice. Of course, there are a few dilettantes who, in the words of a self-confessed member, go from "one brace of snipe to the next."

Nevertheless, they pride themselves on a lack of overt competitive spirit and regard it as a source of strength. "We don't want competition among officers in the mess like the Green Jackets," said a Guards lieutenant colonel. "We want people who fit in. It's like a club, as you know, and it's a happy thing, actually. Looking at our job in Northern Ireland, London and Germany, I place happiness highest of all."

The Guards, therefore, see elitism as a positive force. Another colonel put it this way. "The infantry is not dependent on machines like the cavalry or the artillery so it helps to have a family or a tribe because we are totally dependent on ourselves. Elitism, if you can call it that, is a strength for an army. The army has changed a great deal in the twenty years I have been in but it doesn't change at the same pace as society and perhaps that is not necessarily a bad thing. Our system has proved itself when you are really up against it, when you have to fight, and it works."

Some things, the Guards say, are changing. There is talk of an increasing "Europeanization" of the army. An officer with the Irish Guards in Belize waved his hand towards the jungle-clad mountains and said: "I have no imperial hankerings and I certainly don't want to be a district officer in a place like this, thank you very much." The catchment area for potential officers is widening slowly, mainly under the pressure of shortages, and young men who never would have considered they had a chance before are beginning to come forward.

"We are certainly looking for a wider selection," said another senior officer. "But if you go to the Regular Commissions Board, you'll see how difficult it is. I agree that the British education system is divisive. It is divided into those who have the cash and those who don't. If you've got the cash you can buy a better education. The snag is, it's not just the rich people, it's what you might call the middle class people who impoverish themselves in order to educate their children, and you'll find most of the officers' parents fall into that bracket.

"The RCB says by and large the public schools somehow gear their extramural side to the needs of leadership in the army," he continued. "This is important because in six months these young men can be in Northern Ireland or Belize in the jungle commanding thirty men and if they can't handle it others will suffer."

While Guards officers are aware of the changing world around them and the need for their small, jewelled existence to move forward too if it is to survive they caution against haste. "I think elitism is a fact," said a battalion commander, "and if you are going to change it, like everything else, you change it slowly. I think in a curious way that is precisely what is happening. How do you change it? Well, sometimes you change it through need—like does supply meet the demand? You go to new suppliers and that changes it.

"But it's no good me standing up and saying that we should have X number of secondary [state] schoolboys as officers. That would break up the club. The thirty or so officers in my battalion are a very small, very united body who all know and, I think, all like each other. With newcomers you wouldn't have the same closeness and you'd break that. You'd have to watch the sergeants' mess which is another club and a club which owes its strength to my club, as it were.

"So before you knew where you were," he concluded, "you'd have put a bloody great cleaver through a system far further than you'd wanted. So why not just let it happen, which I think it will. Usually, in time—if a little late in time—things change enough to make sense. So what I am saying is that I don't condemn the present system because I think it has done us bloody well. And I don't entirely endorse it because I think it has to change."

"There is no color bar in the Household Division." Flashback: An army recruiting office in west London where a tall Grenadier Guards color sergeant is explaining the recruiting process. "We accept anyone

if he is over five-foot eight-inches, has a clean record, is of good appearance—assuming he's white of course," (laughs).

"Everyone takes blacks except us," he continues. "As far as I know there will never be a black Guardsman outside Buckingham Palace though I did see a black RAF Regiment sentry there the other day. No blacks have applied to join us here but they have elsewhere and a few complained to the Race Relations Board, I heard.

"How do we stop 'em? Well, what we do is put them through the whole recruiting process, tests, interviews, medical, etcetera. Then if he gets through all that we tell him there are no vacancies in the Household Division at the moment. He is told he can try again later but in the meantime we'll encourage him to join another regiment."

There are no black, brown, or yellow Guardsmen in the fifty-five hundred strong Household Division—Jews and Latins seem to have no problem—although Britain now has two million non-white citizens, many of whom have enlisted in the armed forces. In some infantry regiments—including the Guards' elite rivals, the Royal Green Jackets—the enlistment rate is very high. The underlying Ministry of Defence policy is to keep the rate of non-white recruitment roughly commensurate with the proportion of non-white Britons as a whole, that is at about three and a half percent.

Among the Guards there is a variety of attitudes and a marked vagueness about the screening process that seems to keep the Household Division snow white. In a sense, the Guards' racial reflexes mirror those of many Britons who have not come to terms with, on the one hand, the loss of empire and, on the other, the acquisition of a permanent and growing non-white population that in terms of legal rights and duties, local accents, and general outlook is as British as they are.

Linguistic difficulties, finally resolved in places like the United States through the civil rights movement, show how undigested the problem is. Non-white Britons are variously referred to as "colored people," "coloreds," "immigrants," "West Indians," "Asians," "Paks" or "Pakistanis," "negroes," "blacks," and "browns," and that is leaving aside the perjorative terms. The point was nicely made in a documentary film about the Guards serving in Northern Ireland when the commentator asked the *choggi wallah*—a civilian selling soft drinks and sweets to the soldiers—why had he come all the way from Pakistan to Crossmaglen.

"Actually, I haven't come all the way from Pakistan," the man replied with a smile. "I've come from Birmingham."

Guards officers operate, happily and openly, a double-standard on the issue. "Theoretically, the answer is no colored people apply to join the Household Division," said a senior officer in Germany. "In practice, of course, they do but it is felt that a black or brown face under a bearskin just wouldn't look right."

Another Guards officer said the same thing a slightly different way. "We don't select Guardsmen—they choose us. Totally untrue, of course. But now we're back at the problem of cohesion in a unit, making it work, the happy family idea. It's true other infantry regiments absorb colored recruits but it takes a hell of a lot of time and trouble. The Royal Anglians are about a third colored but they have many problems and their commanding officer has to watch it all the time. Then there's the thing about a black man in a bearskin. The first one would feel a bit of a 'nana,' wouldn't he?"

"Blacks in the Household Division," said a Foot Guards officer, "is a no-no subject. The queen probably wouldn't mind though. There are, I think, some Cypriots and other 'olives' in the Grenadiers and the Coldstream but no blacks. It wouldn't look right with the scarlet tunic, if you see what I mean. They just don't get through though they do apply, I suppose. The problem is dealt with in a typical British fashion—sweep it under the carpet, pretend it's not there. One way of keeping them out, I heard, was the medical officer failing them on their medical. 'Suspected dermatitis.'"

There is an irony in all this. From the middle of the eighteenth century until the middle of the nineteenth century, blacks were regularly employed as musicians in the Household Division. There is also a tradition of foreign "royals" serving for short periods in the Guards, regardless of their skin color. Two of the Sultan of Brunei's sons served in the Foot Guards, as did the Kabaka of Buganda (King "Freddie" Mutesa, as he was called), the Maharajah of Jaipur and Chiang Kai Shek's son.

People further down the line were not so fortunate. There is a story of an olive-skinned Guardsman spotted by a particularly choleric general during a ceremonial inspection at the depot in the early fifties. "Who is he?" barked the general turning a shade darker himself. "An excellent soldier," the officer accompanying him replied. The general glowered. "Fuzzy-wuzzy. Fought 'em. Don't like 'em. Get rid of him." And they did.

The recruiting sergeant was wrong when he said blacks who had applied to join the Guards had complained to the authorities. The Commission for Racial Equality, the Race Relations Board's successor, says it has no complaints of discrimination on record. Guards officers point to the opposition that Guardsmen, particularly the NCO's, have to non-white soldiers joining their ranks though, presumably, if they were admitted, there wouldn't be much that the Guardsmen could do about it.

Two battalion commanders said that, while they were "not all that sorry" about blacks being excluded, they thought they would eventually be admitted. "The Coldstream and the Grenadiers have had people from time to time who have been a bit 'off'," said one of them, "and we have a sergeant who looks Asian but I've never seen a straight black man—or negro—in the Guards." "I personally don't think it will be the end of the world when we do have them in," said the other.

"Homosexuality in the Guards—But what about that Major in the Green Jackets?" "A Guardsman in the park" became a trigger phrase in the popular press many years ago, before the almost medieval laws on homosexuality were changed, and it was usually linked with the name of someone famous or notorious doing something unmentionable. It is not so common now but the imagery lives on and for many people the Guards still suggest rampant homosexuality.

It is, of course, a false impression. In any army or large body of men living and working together there are bound to be some homosexuals. But it may be that there are fewer than one expects because the army comes down heavily on anyone who is revealed as such. "The best way out of the British army," said one Guards officer, "is to say you fancy the chap in the bed next to yours."

One of the main reasons for the publicity the Guards have received in this respect is their highly visible position in London. They are the only military unit that serves regularly in the capital and, as a result of their ceremonial role, anything that happens to them tends to get detailed, sometimes lurid, coverage.

"It's a question of cash," said a lieutenant colonel in the Foot Guards. "There are homosexuals in London with a lot of money and they are prepared to make offers to soldiers who wear high boots in the Household Cavalry for services rendered. If a soldier who is not very well paid and is offered a week's pay in one night, there is always a certain type of person who is going to say yes."

"We have had our problems," said another officer, "but much less so now than a few years ago. I think the change in the law [making homosexual activity between consenting adults legal] has made it easier for people to find other people. And also the soldiers aren't so badly paid now.

"I remember we had a case when I was adjutant back in 1964 when a Guardsman went off into the park with a Member of Parliament who later resigned. And then there was another case a couple of years ago in the Welsh Guards of a lance-corporal who made advances on a Guardsman. The Guardsman was a bit drunk and woke up and found it happening and lashed out. He made a complaint that he was being touched up by this other chap who was court-martialled and left the army."

Homosexuality in the Guards has waxed and waned in direct relation to the financial condition of the soldiers and the climate of the times. In the 1890's, for example, when the pay was bad and Victorian morality was coming apart at the seams, some of the Guards were active in the male brothels of the town. A police raid on one of them revealed that the officers were involved too, including the commanding officer of one of the Household Cavalry regiments, a couple of Dukes and the Prince of Wales.

"I have a fairly enlightened view," said a Foot Guards officer. "After all, homosexuality didn't stop the ancient Greeks from being excellent fighters. If two Guardsmen were messing about together, I wouldn't get too worked up about it . . . it's all good clean fun, quite honestly. But it's very dangerous when senior people do it with junior people.

"In London when a rich person gives a lot of money to a boy," he continued, "it has a terribly corrupting influence on him. Once he has been buggered by someone—he's probably been brought up in a family that finds that quite beyond the pale—and got a taste for the money, his standards are lowered and he will take a totally different attitude towards life."

The last big scandal in the Household Division was in the mid-seventies when twenty men in the Life Guards and a handful in the Blues and Royals were dismissed from the army. "My God," protested an officer in the Household Cavalry when this was brought up, "what about that major in the Green Jackets who, when he was booted out, asked for another 120 cases to be taken into account. That's a whole bloody company!"

South Armagh: Bandit Country

"Regimental loyalty," said a *Times* editorial in 1954, "has always been the British army's unseen reserve." Nowhere is that more true than in the tedious, dangerous and apparently endless campaign against the Irish Republican Army in Northern Ireland.

Regiments are given specific areas to protect and patrol which they do in a high intensity manner for four and a half months at a time. The British army has never been a favorite of the Irish—although many Irishmen join it—a relationship not helped by the Duke of Wellington's comment when asked if he were Irish since he had been born in Dublin. "Not everyone born in a stable," he replied, "is a horse."

The Welsh Guards' headquarters is in Bessbrook, a small, relatively peaceful old mill town founded by a Quaker family and unusual for Ulster in that it has neither public houses nor a police station. The battalion has companies based in other towns throughout the province: Newry, the largest, Newtown Hamilton, the quietest, and Crossmaglen, the worst. Every regiment that has served here since 1974 has had men killed by the IRA.

The most striking thing about South Armagh is the normality of the civilian and the abnormality of the military realities. Walking around Newry or Bessbrook during the end-of-day bustle at five o'clock is a signally unremarkable experience: it is like being in any other small British country town. Living with the Welsh Guards, behind their barricades, is a shock. There really is a war going on around here.

Yet it is a war in which nothing much happens a great deal of the time, a civil war and a war whose end is hull-down over the horizon—on all counts the worst kind of war. It seems to have no redeeming features. There is no money in it—the soldiers get a tiny amount of extra cash for being in Northern Ireland—there is no glory, no social life, no exotica. There is not even much action. The only friends to be made are stray dogs, one of whom, named Rats, has been wounded twice and has become an army celebrity. It's a rough assignment and, as one officer put it, "people's balls drop here."

The helicopter pad at Bessbrook is called "Bessbrook International Heliport" and with reason. The army hardly ever moves by

road. The Wessex is the workhorse helicopter. It carries men—up to eighteen—ammunition and supplies from town to town. The Scout, a much smaller aircraft, is used operationally with two soldiers sitting on either side, the doors open and their feet on the skids ready to leap out as soon as they touch the ground. Then there is the delicate Gazelle, a French helicopter, used for reconnaissance. It swoops low over the countryside following the contours and continuously changing course to avoid being brought down by an IRA rocket.

The choppers also provide the only safe means of travel for army contractors, civilian plumbers and electricians, NAAFI personnel and others who have to get around the treacherous countryside. The Royal Ulster Constabulary's policemen, whose protection is the army's main reason for being here, also rely heavily on these giant metallic insects.

Taxpayers who think the army does not earn its keep should come to South Armagh. The soldiers work enormously hard with twelve-hour to eighteen-hour days not being uncommon. There is no distinction between Saturdays and Sundays and the rest of the week. For four and a half months, apart from a four day "R-and-R" holiday, the regiment is in effect confined to barracks. There are no pubs, cinemas, dances, or outside entertainment of any kind. Television, the occasional film, and working-out in the "multi-gym" are the only diversions from a spartan routine of working, eating, and sleeping.

Apart from patroling on foot in the towns, doing guard duty at the bases, and setting up vehicle checkpoints along country roads, the Welsh Guards send regular patrols deep into the countryside to keep a watch on the border. Their sector is fifty-four miles long and has forty-three border crossings along it. A group of Guardsmen in camouflage uniforms with grease paint—army issue—on their faces, sits waiting for a helicopter to take them out.

They carry their weapons, radios, a checklist of IRA gunmen, and all the food and water they will need for four days in the open. Eighty pounds deadweight. Some will patrol, others will man ambush positions. Either way they will get cold, wet and miserable. If the chopper cannot get back to pick them up because of bad weather they will have to slog back to base across country avoiding the roads which are often mined. We may be in a technological age but the PBI (Poor Bloody Infantry) still have to rely on their feet.

The Welsh Guards are the most tribal of all the Guards regiments. Eighty-five percent are Welshmen, many of the officers too. A quarter of the regiment speak Welsh and the regimental sergeant major, by tradition, is always Welsh-speaking. There are strong family links. One officer, who is leaving soon, says his father was in the regiment and killed during the war. When he joined, many of the NCO's remembered his dad. Now, after seventeen years service, he knows many of their sons. "I am more a Welsh Guardsman than a British soldier," he says and adds sadly, "I shall miss it."

A sergeant on foot patrol in Bessbrook has a list of options for car checks taped onto the stock of his rifle—"border," "republic," "heavy check," and so on. Suspicious car numbers are radioed into the operations room where a check is run on them in Belfast by computer. There are so many Welsh Guardsmen with the same name that they are referred to by numbers, rather like the cars they stop and check in the streets. Thus, "Fifty-six Jones," "Twenty-two Davies," "Eighty-three Griffiths," and so on. So familiar are the numbers that the names are often dropped altogether. "There was once a Jones Double Zero," says an NCO after a couple of drinks in the Sergeants Mess, "who was known as 'Jones Bugger All.'"

South Armagh has green rolling hills with small fields separated by dry stone walls or blackthorn hedges (a source of the Irish Guards officers' rather splendid canes?). It is not unlike the Welsh or Scottish border country with some boggy land, heaths and the occasional copse—a devil to cross at night with eighty pounds on your back. Most of the time it is a quiet and pleasant land where the locals are doing well in farming, small industries, and smuggling, notably pigs that go to and fro across the border collecting government subsidies each time they cross. Yet this land of browsing cows and water meadows erupts with violence and swallows the bloody debris as effortlessly as the ocean engulfs a stricken ship.

The officers' mess is buried in the mortar-proof bosom of the base which is located in the Bessbrook textile mill whose clattering looms gave up the ghost a decade ago. As in other Guards' messes there are the royal portraits, the regimental colors and some silver. The food is pretty good, especially the solid English breakfasts and the fine local stilton cheese. Tea-time has a strong boarding-school flavor with toast, marmite, golden syrup and a variety of not very exciting jams. Living conditions are spartan; small rooms with no daylight, and guest towels the size of a pocket handkerchief. Several officers sport tufts of hair high on their cheekbones, the maximum facial hair—apart from moustaches—allowed by Queen's Regulations. "Bugger's grips," says an officer by way of explanation.

The interminable tours of duty that all regiments—except those of Irish origin—have to do in Northern Ireland seem to lurk in the back of everyone's mind here. Ulster duty used to help recruit in

A visit to a farm by a Welsh Guards patrol (pages 208–209)

the early days but now it has the opposite effect. Each regiment loses some of its men, mainly the younger married ones, when it is slated to return to Ulster. Although the tour itself lasts only four and a half months, several months of training are needed before a regiment sets off and another period is required to settle back into its normal job.

"Household Division training pays off in Northern Ireland," says the commanding officer. "But the word 'discipline' conjures up the wrong image today. It's now self-discipline more than blind obedience. Modern soldiers are much more demanding. Not only will they ask questions during a debriefing but they will also make suggestions. There's no feeling of 'us' and 'them' but the army is a hierarchy and it works best that way. If I start calling a Guardsman by his first name it might work in an exercise when I say, 'Look, Fred, get up that hill, will you?' But it won't work in a war."

Conclusion

"The Guards remain what they are supposed to be," Anthony Sampson wrote in *The Anatomy of Britain* in the mid-sixties, "a superb fighting force: and it is in the army that tribalism and lack of social mobility—so damaging in other fields—have their greatest justification."

Crack force? Yes. Colorful? Yes. Anachronism? No. If there was one phrase we heard more than any other during our travels it was "maintaining our standards." If the Guards are narcissistic, the thrust of their narcissism is to excel in both their roles, as entertainers providing the best pageantry and military music in the business—like any theatrical company they go on tour and make long-playing records—and as fighting troops who will stand when most men run, and retreat—when they must—in good order and with their boots clean.

The military as a whole tends to lag behind the rest of society, wrapped up in its own traditions and preoccupations, and compelled by the dictates of war itself to cling to old-fashioned methods of getting people to do things they are scared to death of doing, like "going over the top" when all hell is breaking loose up there.

But armies also mirror national character and the Guards, although earning their pride of place at the right of the thin red line, have adapted more slowly to modern realities than the rest of the armed forces. In short, while they may be in the van of the army they are in the rear of society.

However, in keeping with the rest of the British establishment which includes the monarchy and aristocracy, the Guards have inched forward sufficiently and escaped the fate of the dodo. Thus they can afford to laugh at themselves—and even be laughed at—because deep down, three hundred years down, in peace and war, in life and death, they know who they are, they know their system works, they know they are a bit better than the rest. They feel secure.

Change, subtly wrought and at a snail's pace, will occur. The balance between ceremonial and operational duties could be altered. While most officers, including the major general, think that balance is about right as it is, others feel the ceremonial should be reduced. During the summer months five battalions—a tenth of the entire British infantry—are tied up in public duties. But organizations like the Foreign and Commonwealth Office and the British Tourist Board are pressing to increase ceremonial, the former wanting it to honor foreign dignitaries and the latter to boost the tourist trade. Ceremonial is important to the Guards beyond the often-stated reasons of tradition, discipline and so on. It ensures their survival as we now know them. A significant reduction in their ceremonial role or its abolition altogether would, in effect, make them much more like the normal line infantry and cavalry regiments and leave them equally vulnerable to amalgamation and even, in an extreme situation, to disbandment.

Change will also probably bring the broadening of the officer corps. There may one day be a black Guardsman on duty outside Buckingham Palace and private incomes could totally disappear as a "helpful" factor in the officer recruitment process. After all, who would have thought some time ago that new recruits would be treated with kid gloves during their early days at the depot, that young ensigns would be talked to on their first day in the mess, and that "new-fangled" things like cocktails would be served before lunch?

In the final analysis, the Guards' survival is linked with that of the monarchy. They are the sovereign's guards—although the police do most of the guarding these days—that's how they started and that is still their greatest strength, the thing that makes them different from other old and prestigious units in the British army. The queen, who personally plays a major part in selecting their general and who takes a detailed interest in their activities—she reports Guardsmen who are improperly dressed or "idle" on parade—has shown no signs of wanting to get rid of them. Nor has her eventual successor, Prince Charles. The Guards, from the way they talk, give the impression that they will always be around. And, whether you admire them or not, they are probably right.

The Irish border, green and deadly. Welsh Guards airborne patrol (pages 212–213)

Part VI

Portraits

The Guards are a closely knit family. And yet those who have served with them seem to be everywhere, to have permeated all of British society, especially at the leadership level.

That maroon-and-navy striped Guards tie is a low-keyed but ubiquitous reminder of their upward mobility. Former members of the Guards are found in Parliament, in the Foreign Office and the Treasury, in the Stock Exchange and corporate boardrooms, in the schools and universities, in the church, in industry, and in farming.

There has been a great leveling in the social structure of Britain since the end of the Second World War. Certain institutions, however, retain their elitist image and their power to influence the career of alumni. The top public schools—Eton, Harrow, Winchester, and so on—and the ancient universites of Oxford and Cambridge are prime examples in the civilian sphere. The Guards fulfill that function in the military.

We have chosen—not scientifically, but, we hope, judiciously enough to show the breadth of the Guards experience—six people who spent their formative years in the Guards and who have been successful in different walks of life, including the army itself.

They are: Major General Adair; Lord Carrington; Viscount de L'Isle; Earl of Lichfield; Robert Runcie, Archbishop of Canterbury; and Colonel David Stirling.

Major Neil Ramsay, ex-Scots Guards, on his grouse moor at Aberfeldy, Scotland (page 215)

Major General
Sir Allan Adair

Geneneral Adair, the old soldier, lives with his wife in a red-brick town house in Mayfair, close to Hyde Park. The house is high Victorian Gothic, built by Cubitt in the 1890's. Inside, it is rather gloomy, crowded with heavy period furniture, art treasures, military memorabilia, and personal bric-a-brac: an antiquarian's Aladdin's cave. The couple are in their eighties, immaculately dressed, spry, and welcoming.

On the staircase walls and in the first-floor drawing room there are many Reynolds portraits and a number of landscapes by Flemish painters. Leatherbound works of Dickens, Thackeray, Byron, and Scott fill the bookshelves in neat Guardslike ranks. In the General's dressing room his frock coat, tunic, and medals hang on a hat stand; beside them lie his silver-backed hairbrushes and combs.

Beneath, completing the military still life, are his riding boots: old leather gleaming in the Victorian twilight.

He offers us a glass of sherry as we talk in the ground-floor study, which is protected from the noise of London's traffic by heavy velvet curtains. On an elegant rosewood table are a tray of smoking accessories—a silver cigar cutter, a cigarette holder, snuffboxes—and a pile of books. Field Marshal Montgomery's memoirs lie on top, but lower down, somewhat surprisingly, lies a copy of *Private Eye*.

"I think I am in the unique position," General Adair begins crisply, "of being the only surviving Grenadier officer to have fought in both world wars."

Born shortly after his house was built, Adair was educated at Harrow and joined the Third Battalion Grenadier Guards in France in 1916. He was wounded twice, the second time just before the Armistice in November, 1918, and, as it happened, on his twenty-first birthday. His intention had been to go up to Oxford after the war, but he decided to stay on as a regular officer. And, in one way or another, General Adair has been with his beloved regiment ever since.

217.

"My family came over from Scotland to Ulster and settled around Ballymena. I have the original lease from King James I, in which it says my ancestor William Adair could hold the market on the 'fair hills in order to civilize the wild and unruly inhabitants.' I don't think we have done it yet, do you? Would you like some more sherry? Yes, of course, do smoke. I am going to smoke my pipe. Now, where were we?"

The General had an ancestor in the Grenadiers who was killed at Waterloo, but after that none of his family served with the Guards until his own time. However, he seems to have made up for it. His only son was in the Grenadiers and was killed in Italy during the Second World War. He has one daughter married to a Coldstream officer and another married to an officer in the Irish Guards.

The Second World War was a time of swift advancement for Adair. He began it as a major and ended it as a general, commanding the famed Guards Armored Division. He fought at Dunkirk and returned to France with his division in the D-Day landings.

"It was a strange thing," he says, "for what we considered to be the best infantry in the world suddenly to have to become expert about tanks. Our first problem was fitting our large Guardsmen into the small driver's seats, but by the time the invasion came we had sorted everything out."

(Interruption as a maid rushes in to say that Lady Adair, who had gone to buy Christmas cards at Smiths in Oxford Street, is pinioned by the wind in the shop's entrance. Every time she ventures forth, the maid says breathlessly, she gets blown back in again. Support troops in the guise of a photographer and art director are dispatched to the West End front.)

"When we crossed the Channel there was a terrible storm," the General continues. "The pontoon carrying my car and all my kit for the campaign, including a case of champagne—I hate going to war unprepared—was washed away down the French coast. We found it later, untouched and in good working order, in the Canadians' drowned vehicle park.

"We were held up at Caen and had an unpleasant time in our first taste of tank warfare. Then we were on the move again, and I shall never forget the excitement of giving orders to my brigade commanders to advance and capture Brussels. It was a hundred miles away, but we were off, flying through Arras, where I had won my Military Cross in the First War. It became a race between our two columns, the Grenadiers on the right and the Welsh Guards on the left, which the Welsh won by a short head."

218.

Major General Sir Allan Adair Bt., GCVO, CB, DSO, MC, JP, DL; late Grenadier Guards

Then came Arnhem. "It was hopeless for tanks," Adair says, puffing at his pipe. "There was only one road to Arnhem, with polder land, either under water or very soft, on each side. Anyway, we finally forced our way through to Nijmegen and down to the great bridge over the Waal with some very brave battling. Peter Carrington [Lord Carrington, Foreign Secretary] went over with his tanks and we counted seventy dead and a hundred and twenty prisoners on the bridge itself after the battle. Meanwhile, the Americans did a marvelously brave crossing lower down the river in collapsible boats they had never used before.

"However, it was the railway bridge that they captured, not the road bridge, which was an entirely Grenadier affair. That's where the film [*A Bridge Too Far*] got it wrong. It was also wrong on Lieutenant General 'Boy' Browning, who they made out to be rather weak and irresponsible. Quite the contrary, he was a brave and gallant man."

(The front door opens and excited voices are heard. "Are you back, darling?" the General cries. Lady Adair, a diminutive, birdlike woman, enters the room. "Yes, I'm back. I thought I would never get back." The support troops, who literally performed that function, one on either side of the old lady, refresh themselves with a sherry and a bag of potato chips that the General has handy.)

After the war, Adair retired from the army but took over the Yeomen of the Guard—"the Beefeaters, as everyone wrongly calls them." He also followed in the footsteps of Marlborough and Wellington by becoming Colonel of the Grenadier Guards and was for a time Deputy Grand Master of the United Grand Lodge of Freemasons.

Having fought in both world wars, General Adair is well qualified to compare them. "The Second War was absolutely cushy compared with the First," he says. "On the western front we stood for days up to our armpits in water with the Boche only thirty or forty yards away from those awful communication trenches. How people survived I just don't know."

And the Guards? "The relationship between the NCO's and officers is much closer now than in my early days. The men are much better educated, more intelligent, and I think the teamwork is more pronounced. There is a lot to be said for the Guardsmen. . . . There are other splendid units in the British army, of course there are, but I think there is something about a Guardsman that is, well, unique."

220.

Lord Carrington

The scene is Washington in its May cloak of azaleas—rose, white and a rather shocking "day-glo" red—with the pungent smell of fresh mown grass in the air. Lord Carrington, Foreign Secretary, arrived the night before on a Concorde jet from London and is staying in the British Ambassador's residence. Today, he is catching up on his paperwork, appearing on American television programs, and when he has a spare moment, reminiscing about his days in Her Majesty's Foot Guards. Tomorrow, he will be immersed in the affairs of state, as is proper for the successful politician that he has turned out to be.

The embassy residence on Massachusetts Avenue, built by Sir Edwin Lutyens, the great architect of the British raj in India, is as stunning as the chancery building, designed by Sir Basil Spence, is dismal. While we wait at the head of the grand staircase outside the ambassador's study where Lord Carrington is planning his day, a swift flies in pursued by flustered servants in blue and white striped aprons.

"They often get in at this time of year," says one of them waiting for the panic-striken bird to settle. "It's the oil paintings we're worried about it." He points to the huge portraits of British monarchs that adorn the walls. They go back to King George III who, of course, was responsible for an embassy being here in the first place.

The study door opens and we are ushered in. Somewhere in the depths of the building a telephone rings, two insistent rings—a British sound and quite different the single plaintive American tone. Lord Carrington is a small man with hornrimmed spectacles and a ready laugh. He orders some coffee, sits down in a high-backed winged chair, and talks about how he came to join the Guards.

"The only thing I wanted as a young man was to have a political life," he says. "But it's extremely difficult to say so when you are aged sixteen. My father said, well, if you don't know what you want to do you'd better go into the Grenadiers where he and my grandfather had been. So I went to Sandhurst in 1937 but I think I missed a lot by not going to university though as it turned out I would never have finished because of the war. Sandhurst was very tough in those days. I remember the first time I laid out the screws and springs of my rifle for inspection the senior under-officer found it dirty, picked up the sheet they were spread out on and chucked the whole thing out of the window. I suppose it taught you a certain sort of humility and patience and acceptance of what on the surface was a rather odd way of behaving."

Having a family tradition in the Grenadiers, Carrington did not have much difficulty joining the regiment. The adjutant at Sandhurst at that time was a friend of his father's—they had fought in the First World War together—and the lieutenant colonel commanding the regiment was his cousin. "I've no doubt that was disgraceful," Carrington says with a smile, "but that's how it was in those days. I don't think it's that way now." He joined the Grenadiers in Wellington Barracks in January, 1939 and spent much of his spare time during his first six months there writing letters. "No one talked to you," he says, "so I just sat in the anteroom writing letters."

Like many former Guards officers, Carrington has a "disaster" tale from his time doing ceremonial duties. "The first time I went on guard at Buckingham Palace was with an old friend from school [Eton]. We thought we had prepared for every conceivable eventuality but while we were walking up and down carrying the colors, Princess Elizabeth and Princess Margaret came out of an inner courtyard in a motor car. Neither of us had the smallest idea of what we were supposed to do so we had a hurried consultation. My friend said he thought we had better go on and pretend nothing had happened. I said we can't possibly do that—obviously something *had* happened—we'd better stand to attention and lower the color. He disagreed and said he was going on, do what you like. So he marched on and I stood to attention and lowered the color. We were both wrong and both of us got into the most appalling trouble."

Life as a peacetime officer just before the Second World War was easy-going but even when the Guards went on training exercises they were hampered by lack of weapons. "We had no machine guns and during exercises we had to use different flags to show we were firing our anti-tank rifles or our Bren guns. And when we did get weapons they weren't very good."

Carrington did not go to France in the early stages of the war because he was under twenty-one years of age but in the summer of 1940 he was sent down to the small arms school in Hythe in Kent. "During the day we trained as the dogfights went on over the Channel and at night we guarded the beaches," he says sipping his coffee. "We

had three and a half miles of beach between Hythe and Folkestone to protect and with forty-eight men, three Bren guns, and a pistol. We would sit there all night waiting for the German invasion. It's extraordinary looking back on it. . . . It simply never occurred to me that if the Germans arrived we wouldn't push them back into the sea. I thought, you know, it's bad luck on the Germans if they come, they're going to have a terrible time!"

For the next three years Carrington shared the frustration of other Guardsmen who were being transformed into the Guards Armored Division. "It took time to 'train out' the blind obedience of the Guards system because now our requirements were different," he says. "With three or four men in a tank, personal initiative is very much needed. To give you an example, I had a marvelous squadron sergeant major, a great tall man, but when I used to call him on the radio there was always a long pause. One day I was near enough to see what was happening. When he heard my voice on the radio, he would salute first then pick up the microphone. Also the old Grenadier custom of saying only 'Sir' to any question took a lot of getting rid of."

Carrington fought with the Guards Armored Division across northwestern Europe until the war ended with Germany's surrender. He won the Military Cross and led the first tanks across the Nijmegen bridge in the abortive attempt to link up with airborne troops in Arnhem. He has few memories of that bitter campaign—"I am ashamed to say I have neither read Cornelius Ryan's book *A Bridge Too Far* nor seen the film"—but he does recall the bravery of the RAF pilots who had to resupply the armored column even though they were sitting targets for the Germans. And he does value the time spent in the Guards: "Comradeship in war obviously has an effect upon you and how you think. And social divisions disappear when you share your life with three other people in a tank. I'll never forget the brave, splendid people I served with."

After the war, Lord Carrington launched himself on a political career. He held junior ministerial posts in Winston Chruchill's and Anthony Eden's governments, and was High Commissioner in Australia, leader of the Conservative party in the House of Lords in the sixties, and Defence Minister in Edward Heath's government. As Foreign Secretary under Margaret Thatcher, he negotiated the settlement of the Rhodesia-Zimbabwe crisis after long months of tightrope diplomacy. The settlement led to an end of the country's seven-year-long civil war. All pretty impressive for a man whose only "university" training was eighteen months of square-bashing and rifle cleaning at Sandhurst.

Viscount De L'Isle, VC

If William Philip Sidney—Lord De L'Isle—did not exist there would be a case for inventing him, for he is a perfect cameo of the British aristocrat. His lineage is impeccable, his service to the Crown lengthy and honorable. He has a stately home in Kent and a flat in Belgravia. He went to Eton and Cambridge and he served in the Grenadier Guards. He is the only living holder of the highest military and civil awards in Britain: the Victoria Cross and the Garter. It is easy to typecast him as a peer of the realm or a military hero—or both. He, more modestly, likes to refer to himself as "a man of public affairs."

"When I was six or seven I remember my father saying that the then Lieutenant Colonel of the Grenadiers had suggested he should put my name down for the regiment, which he duly did." The young De L'Isle did not think much more about the army until he was at Cambridge, when he decided to join the supplementary reserve. "I was pessimistic about a war coming and I wanted to know who I would be fighting alongside. So there I was, over fifty years ago, a young and rather ingenuous undergraduate wearing a bowler hat and a stiff collar, as I had been advised, walking into the orderly room of the Grenadier Guards in Wellington Barracks.

"I can see it now. I was ushered into a room that was full of Turkish tobacco smoke and through it I saw a man with piercing blue eyes sitting behind a desk smoking a cigarette. I stood to attention and he asked me why I wanted to join the regiment, and I explained in rather halting, callow terms. I was accepted on June 22, 1929, and gazetted at the beginning of July." De L'Isle then served for ten years on the reserve and was a captain when war broke out in September, 1939. "The only medal I had at that stage," he says, "was the St. John of Jerusalem, which the Guardsmen used to say was awarded for gallantry in the blackout." Today, Lord De L'Isle's decorations include the VC, KG, PC, GCMG, GCVO—cryptography to the uninitiated, but a roll of honor to the cognoscenti.

The family connection with the Guards goes back to 1693, when an ancestor, Henry Sidney, became the third Colonel of the Grenadiers. "However, between that time and my joining the regiment," Lord De L'Isle continues, "there was a long interregnum. My great-grandfather was in the Life Guards. My grandfather, who was in the Blues, put one of his sons into the Rifle Brigade and another into the Royal Artillery. My father was born in 1859 and so missed all the great wars. It is a curious thing in my family that we have timed our successive generations to miss all the major wars. Until they caught up with me." De L'Isle's son and heir, one need hardly add, is in the Grenadier Guards.

During the war De L'Isle was in the retreat from Dunkirk and was later sent to North Africa and Italy. He returned to Britain in 1944 to prepare for the Normandy landings but found himself "diverted" to the House of Commons, where he joined Winston Churchill's government as a junior minister.

"That's my military history, which, apart from one notorious episode, was very undistinguished."

Would he like to talk a little about that "notorious episode"?

"Not particularly," De L'Isle says. "I think I was extremely lucky. The attention of the world was concentrated on the landing at Anzio, but it didn't go as well as it was hoped and I happened to be at a particular place at a particular time when everyone was anxious that the Germans shouldn't get through. So, with a good deal of literary effort and a certain amount of press detail, I suppose somebody had to get it [the Victoria Cross] and I got it. When people ask where were you wounded, I always say I was wounded in Italy. They then say no, but where exactly, and I have to confess I was wounded in the bottom."

De L'Isle's political career blossomed during Churchill's second government, when he was appointed Air Minister. "I was astonished when Churchill told me," he said. "I then asked him if he knew what had happened to the last member of my family who had held high office. He said he didn't. I told him it was Henry Sidney, who had been sacked by the Duke of Marlborough, who was Churchill's ancestor, of course. He looked at me and said, 'Was he a Whig?' I said he was. He said, 'Well, you're a Tory now.'"

De L'Isle later became Governor-General of Australia. He is still active as a businessman, philanthropist, and chairman of the National Association for Freedom.

What does he think of his time in the Household Division?

"The army gives you a form of thought," he replies. "You

Colonel The Rt. Hon. Viscount De L'Isle VC, KG, GCMG, GCVO, PC, JP, DL; late Grenadier Guards

don't really put up with second class easily. On the other hand, you can never be 'under the impression' about anything. Either you know or you don't know. And if you don't know you go and find out. It's just, but not fair. Do you understand what I mean? You sometimes get blamed for something that's not your fault, but somebody has to be blamed and you learn to take it.

"What do I feel about the Grenadier Guards in particular? Well, Harold Macmillan, who served in the Grenadiers in the First World War, put it much better than I ever could. He said, 'It is a great thing at some time in your life to be associated with something which is quite first class.' That's precisely how I feel."

Earl of Lichfield

The scene is a photographer's studio in a quiet corner of Kensington not far from Holland Park. The walls are black and white, with leaded windows in the front facing the street, and picture windows in the rear overlooking a peaceful English garden. There are tubular steel chairs with gray cord cushions, a hi-fi, stacks of film and developing paper ready for use, and tools neatly arrayed on wall racks. A map of the world with a mass of colored pins—different colors for different continents, each pin representing a location shoot—hangs on one wall.

In his early forties, Lichfield is good-looking and relaxed. He wears a fair amount of gold: signet ring, wrist chain, and neck chain. He has a pleasant voice and a knack for making people feel comfortable. He is very conscious of being a photographer first and everything else second, which is not to say "everything else" doesn't matter.

When you telephone him his secretary answers, "Patrick Lichfield's studio." But then, you would hardly expect her to say, "Thomas Patrick John Anson, Viscount Anson and Baron Soberton, Fifth Earl of Lichfield." And there would be absolutely no reason for her to add that her employer is a relative of the Queen and married to Lady Leonora Grosvenor, daughter of the Duke of Westminster, or that he was educated at Harrow School and served in the Grenadier Guards. "My grandfather wasn't in the regiment, but my father served for twenty-two years and all my uncles had been in the Grenadiers. I had to go into the army anyway because of National Service, but I signed on for five years when I was at Sandhurst although I already had a strong yen to be a photographer."

What was it like in the Guards in the late fifties?

"It was extremely exciting to realize that we were very professional. It was tough, with very little time for relaxation, but the pluses were enormous. Sandhurst was an interesting experience because there you had a lot of young men being kicked into excellence. The Guards either got absolutely top or absolutely bottom marks in everything.

"The NCO's were marvelous. There is no other regimental system that depends so enormously on the excellence of the NCO's. My own company Sergeant Major when I was in the regiment was a total hero figure. He later became Academy Sergeant Major at Sandhurst. Jack Lord held that job in my day.

"I remember one day Lord had us all marched into the academy theater and told us that we were going to have a little lecture on the media by Mr. Eamon Andrews, who promptly walked on and said, 'Sergeant Major Lord, this is your life!' Lord stood rigidly to attention and saluted him."

The Guards, especially the Grenadiers, used to be renowned for the cool reception they gave to new officers, didn't they?

"Adjutants could be quite terrifying. I had the advantage of having quite a lot of relations in the regiment and of knowing beforehand that I would be received frostily. So I didn't make the terrible error my father did when he walked into the mess and said it was going to be a nice day. Somebody stood up and announced, 'Lord Anson wishes to address the mess on the weather.' That really shut him up.

"But I do remember that after dinner on my first night in the mess, brandy snaps were served up with some kind of cream dessert. I had trouble breaking one. When it finally gave way, half of it flew

229.

upwards, spreading cream over my chest, and the other piece snaked down the table and landed on the Commanding Officer's lap.

"The social structure is pretty rigid and the language quite extraordinary. It's interesting going back and having lunch at St. James's Palace and hearing them using the same old colloquialisms like people being 'idle' or 'bolo.' And when it comes to things like sexual conquests, they are actually quite quaint. They always seem to be slightly behind: they will be talking about 'birds' when everyone else is talking about 'chicks.'

"And yet," Lichfield continues, "some of the more intelligent and enlightened officers are extra-special people. Also, some of my contemporaries who are still in have told me that the requirements for being a successful army officer are much tougher than what they were ten or fifteen years ago.

"Of course, for me there was a rather superficial feeling of protection in the Guards. I don't think I ever had such a bump as when I came to terms with reality after the army. I left on October fourteenth, 1962, at two-thirty p.m. and I was plunged into instant penury because my mother was so upset—as were the family trustees— that I should forsake what seemed to be a fairly promising career for what, in those days, was regarded as a pretty ignominious career. I found myself working for three pounds a week as a photographic assistant, and *that* was the tough one. Suddenly, the car had to go, I had to get a bike, and I had to do all my own laundry, clean my shoes and so on—all of which I wasn't used to."

Do you keep in touch?

"Nearly everyone I met in the Guards and became friendly with remained friends. I am president of the local branch of the Old Comrades Association. There is an extraordinary affinity. . . . If I see a chap with a red-and-blue tie in the Underground I will ask him what regiment he was with. . . . It's a very strong thing. As a photographer I am possibly seen as rather an oddball, though not so much now, perhaps because I've calmed down a bit.

"I have a son, and it is my fervent hope that, conscription or not, he will go into the regiment."

Did you put his name down?

Lichfield laughs. "The day after he was born I got an application form from the regimental adjutant, saying 'Time is not to be wasted.' They had seen in the paper that the Countess of Lichfield had given birth to a son."

What about the ceremonial: a blessing or a scourge?

"I did two years of it, which was hilariously funny and fright-

Lord Patrick The Earl of Lichfield

fully boring. Of course, one got up to terrible tricks. There was one man, ten days senior to me, who had disliked me from the day I first met him at Sandhurst. He did some unpleasant things to me and generally made my life uncomfortable. So I devised a method whereby his servant, who didn't seem to like him much either, and I managed to secrete a large kitchen alarm clock in his bearskin and set it for the precise moment when the Horse Guards came past as he was presenting arms outside Buckingham Palace. We didn't warn the other Guardsmen, and it went off right on time in the top of his head. Everyone was convulsed and he was very cross."

Robert Runcie, Archbishop of Canterbury

At the entrance to the House of Lords we are greeted by Doorkeeper T. Taylor, resplendent in white tie and tails, but arguably more resplendent—and certainly more powerful—in his previous incarnation as Garrison Sergeant Major T. Taylor (Grenadier Guards), London District.

Robert Runcie, Archbishop of Canterbury, leads us to the Lower Bishops' Changing Room. It is a paneled Victorian room with cupboards stuffed with episcopal robes and fireplace andirons that have miters embossed on them. There are two bishops per cupboard, and Hereford and Exeter, cupboard partners, drop in at different times to change their robes. There are occasional crashes outside, as if someone is systematically, and with a good deal of relish, destroying government property.

Runcie wears a gray suit, dog collar, and a heavy silver cross over his port-colored shirt. He looks a little like a younger version of the actor Alistair Sim. He has a light-timbred voice, a delicate sense of humor, and muscular convictions: a modern man of the church.

He joined the army during the early stages of the war, while he was at Oxford. He thought he would enlist with the King's Own Scottish Borderers because his father was a Scot. But then he was approached by the adjutant of the Scots Guards. "I told him that I imagined I would have to have ancestry and an income for that," Runcie says.

"He turned to his assistant and said, 'I don't think you need all that much private income, do you?' And that was that. But the surprising thing was the way in which I, as an outsider, was accepted by the other officers."

Runcie joined the famous Third Battalion in the Guards Armored Division, the unit that launched so many stars into different firmaments in the postwar years. He served from 1941 to 1946 and won the Military Cross for dashing across open ground, through heavy German enfilading fire, to drag one of his men from a burning tank and carry him back to safety.

What did he get out of his time in the Guards?

"I was a bit all over the place when I joined them. It pulled me together. It not only gave me a sort of assurance, which could be dangerous because it's always toppling into arrogance, but it also gave me a sort of idealism."

Idealism?

"Yes. Service to the sovereign and country. Courage that doesn't waver when the going is tough. All those kind of things are formalized in the Guards. Now, I do not share most of the political and social views of my Guards friends, but I shall always be grateful for the way in which integrity, idealism and sticking to the things you believed in were genuinely respected behind all the banter and the privilege.

"I think I had the best of both worlds," the Archbishop continues. "I didn't come from that Guards elite, yet I was accepted into it. I will admit I have acquired some Guardee manners of speech and habit which no doubt create a gulf when I go to talk to shop-floor trades unionists in a factory or go to a football match. When I claim that I am a lad who was brought up in Liverpool and my father was just an ordinary electrical engineer, they look at me and think, 'He's putting it on.'".

Have the Guards changed much over the years?

"Yes, they have undoubtedly changed, though it is interesting that the same families are still there. Recently, I went to preach at the passing-out parade at Sandhurst and although the place has been transformed physically by technology, I thought it was very much the same as in my day. Even my Sergeant-Major—living in retirement—was still there."

How does he reconcile the pursuit of war and religion?

"Any man of the church who doesn't have a bit of a pain in his mind about being a man of war has got his Christianity in funny proportions. But, after all, I was hardly a Christian in those days. I don't think there is any place for the clergy in the fighting line. However, I still hold to the simple truth there are, in terms of human indignity, worse things than war and that sometimes it is the lesser of two evils."

Colonel David Stirling

The man behind the oak desk could be in his early fifties; he has a strong face, piercing, slightly mischievous blue eyes, and graying hair.

"How nice to see you," he says, standing up. "Will you have a cup of tea or perhaps some of the hard stuff?" He waves a large hand at a liquor cabinet in the corner of the room. We sit down on a sofa facing a bow window with leaded panes which looks out over a discreet Mayfair courtyard in the heart of London. Colonel David Stirling folds his six-foot-six-inch body into an armchair and chats about parachuting behind Rommel's lines in the western desert and doing nasty things to the Germans, who rarely knew what hit them. He talks as if it were yesterday instead of forty years ago.

"That was how the SAS began," he says, referring to his brainchild, Britain's Special Air Service, the elite commando force whose emblem is the winged dagger and whose function remains collecting intelligence and causing mayhem deep in enemy territory. "We used jeeps a lot. Marvelous vehicles. The principle was to drive like hell at night and lie low during the day. The further behind Jerry's front line the better. Would you care for some more tea?"

Stirling is, in fact, in his mid-sixties. He owns vast estates in Scotland, hunts, shoots, and fishes, and sounds as if he has stepped out of the pages of John Buchan, perhaps *The Thirty-nine Steps*. The sign on his office door says "International Television Enterprises," and, among other things, his company dubs *Sesame Street* into Arabic and sells it profitably to the oil sheikhdoms of the Persian Gulf. The "other things" are more interesting if less visible and include the provision of bodyguards for foreign heads of state, soldiers of fortune for remote wars, and, occasionally, an SAS-style combat team for a wealthy and ideologically acceptable client.

The telephone rings. Stirling moves agilely and answers it.

"It was a funny thing, you know," he says, returning to his chair and lighting a Havana cigar. "When we got to France we found out where Rommel was staying, and one of our chaps had him in his sights every day. But we had orders not to shoot. Rather bad news for a chap trained to kill, what? You've got *Numero Uno* in your sights and you can't do a damned thing about it!" He laughs boyishly. "Why? Well, it seemed there were two reasons. First, we knew all about Rommel by then—how he handled his troops, the way he would react in a given situation, and so on. It was a case of the devil you know. . . . And then we also suspected he wasn't all that keen on the management. Do help yourselves, the whiskey's in the decanter."

After countless raids and adventures in the desert, Stirling was captured by the Italians, escaped, captured by the Germans, escaped and recaptured, taken to Italy, escaped once again, and finally sent to Colditz, where he remained for the rest of the war. "It was a bit tricky, you see," he says, sipping his tea. "I'd get out all right, but being a fully grown chap and not speaking a word of the lingo, I didn't stay out very long."

He was decorated for valor and emerged from the war as one of Britain's most colorful military heroes. Like many other Britons in prominent walks of life, David Stirling began his career in the Guards.

Stirling is the middle son of a well-to-do Scottish family from Keir in Stirlingshire and, like his two brothers, was educated at Ampleforth and Cambridge. He did quite well at the Catholic public school, but his thoughts were on other things by the time he got to Trinity College, Cambridge, where he spent a lot of time and money at the Newmarket races. After university he decided that he was going to be the first man to climb Mount Everest but acknowledged that he would have to put in some serious training. Accordingly, in 1938, he went to Canada, bought three horses, and set off on an ambitious ride south along the continental divide, stopping to climb mountains on the way. A year earlier he had started part-time training with the Scots Guards at Pirbright in Surrey, but his military commitment seems to have slipped his mind when he embarked on his great American trek.

When the war broke out, he had done about two thousand miles on horseback and had reached Jackson Hole, Wyoming, living off the country and practicing his climbing skills.

"I had a bet with a friend that I would climb twenty mountains over ten thousand feet, but the war stopped me cleaning up," he says, puffing at his cigar. "Fortunately, it also prevented me from getting into serious trouble for missing my military training."

Why did he join the Scots Guards? "Well, my father had been in the regiment and my two brothers, Bill and Hugh, were in it. An inevitable choice." His penchant for the energetic and the exotic was almost immediately gratified when it was announced that a ski battalion was being formed—it became the Fifth Battalion of the Scots Guards, the "Snowballers"—to fight in Scandinavia. "We did our training in Chamonix and so got a skiing holiday after all. But when the Finns capitulated and the Germans conquered Norway, the whole scheme was canceled. Nevertheless, it had been a useful experience because I finished up as a sergeant, which is a very privileged place to be in the Guards in view of the considerable insulation between the officers and the other ranks."

He then joined Robert Laycock's commando unit as a newly commissioned ensign. The commando, the first of its kind in the British army, was raised from the Brigade of Guards exclusively, and many of the officers, it is said, were recruited from the bar in White's Club. Stirling emphasizes the importance of the Guards NCO's. "The drill sergeants were kind but exceedingly firm with young green officers like me, and when you went on parade they used to put you next to someone who had a name roughly similar to your own. I remember there was a Guardsman called Starling who was excellent at drill. He was put beside me and sworn at solidly throughout by the drill sergeant, although it was quite clear who in fact the sergeant was referring to."

Stirling fought with Laycock's commando in the Middle East until the unit was disbanded after Rommel's lightning victories and the fall of Crete. However, Stirling remained convinced that there was a role for commando-style operations, though on a much smaller scale. He worked out a plan which in that day and age could only be described as revolutionary. Laycock's commandos had operated in large groups of a minimum of two hundred men and usually approached their targets from the sea and were thus dependent on the navy. Stirling now proposed a much smaller, highly trained specialist outfit operating in groups of four or five men. Each group would be dropped behind the enemy lines by parachute or get there by jeep under the cover of darkness and attack vulnerable targets such as airfields, vehicle parks and ammunition dumps.

He had already started to experiment with parachuting and had ended up in hospital with both legs temporarily paralyzed. The enforced rest imposed by the injury gave him time to perfect his ideas. Then came the task of implementation, no easy feat for a young ensign confronted with the dead weight of the British military bureaucracy in Cairo in the torrid summer of 1941.

Stirling, although still on crutches, managed to slip past the sentry and get into military headquarters, which proved to be the easiest part of the operation. He opened the first door he came to and encountered a major who remembered Stirling from his days with the Scots Guards: Stirling was the one who always fell asleep on the major's lectures. After listening to the major's objections to his plan, Stirling saluted and departed. Then he tried another door, marked DCGS. Inside the door was General Ritchie, Deputy Commander Middle East. Philip Warner, in his book *The Special Air Service*, describes what happened next: "Stirling apologized for his unannounced arrival, gave a brief explanation for his visit and handed over an outline plan for the general to study. Ritchie took a brief look at it, thought for a moment, then announced that he would discuss the plan with the Commander-in-Chief and summon Stirling for a conference if necessary. This interview is held by many to be Stirling's greatest achievement, it being one thing to defeat the Germans, but another thing entirely to brush bureaucracy to one side."

Within three days of the interview with Ritchie, Stirling found himself in the presence of the Commander-in-Chief, General Auchinleck, who had replaced Wavell after Rommel's triumphant sweep through the desert. Stirling was given the go-ahead, promoted to captain, and told he would come under the direct authority of Au-

chinleck himself. He had permission to recruit six officers and sixty NCO's and men. Since most came from Laycock's No. 8 Commando, the majority were Guardsmen—Scots, Grenadiers and Coldstreamers principally.

In a typical piece of British obscurantism, Stirling was informed that his unit would be known as "L Detachment" of the "Special Air Service Brigade." There was, in fact, no such thing as the SAS, much less a brigade; the name existed merely as a decoy to lead the Germans into believing British paratroops had arrived in the Middle East. An enterprising brigadier had been busily dropping dummy soldiers and leaving dummy gliders on airfields for the benefit of enemy reconnaissance. The SAS was a phantom force, but it was soon to assume a human form of the most menacing kind under the leadership of its young creator.

Colonel Stirling lifts his large frame out of his chair and walks across to the fireplace. "The big problem," he says, "was getting commanding officers to let their best men go, and we became fairly crafty about extricating them. We aimed at top standards in drill, turnout and kit, et cetera, but also laid an enormous stress on training. A new officer would be under the command of a sergeant until he had proved himself. We also promoted NCO's to officer rank in the field because we didn't want to lose a particularly good man to officer training school. This was not done in any other unit, as far as I know. I have always been opposed to any sense of class, and there never was class feeling in the SAS. We were very democratic, and I never had any hesitation in putting a young officer under a sergeant."

A number of well-known people served in the SAS, including Randolph Churchill, son of the wartime Prime Minister. "Winston rather approved of me," Stirling says with a grin, "because I was always throwing Randolph out of airplanes."

Stirling thinks the exacting standards set by the Guards were highly relevant to the success of the SAS in the field. "A lot of the Guards prewar training was not war-related," he says. "But the standards they had to attain, especially the high level of discipline, meant that when they came to a war situation they were very reliable soldiers. They were particularly responsive to command, and one reason why they had such enormous casualties was that whenever there was trouble they were liable to be sent for; and the reason for that was the high expectations of their performance."

One of Stirling's secretaries—they seem to have "county" names like Rachel and Cynthia—comes in with his "libel file." He is often the target of the left-wing press, which sees him as a latter-day

Cold Warrior, trying vainly to stem the communist tide by nefarious means at home and abroad. He has three cases pending—he usually wins, with "substantial" damages being awarded to him—and one of them, he says with a laugh, turns on an accusation that he was plotting to kill the Kenyan President, Vice-President, and half the cabinet.

Stirling's active military career came to an end when he was captured in 1943. The first time he managed to escape quite easily. "We were kept in a garage, but they had to let us out to deal with the call of nature, to shake it out, and so forth. Well, I just kept on going."

The next time he wasn't so fortunate. The Germans had formed a special unit to tackle the SAS. During the final training exercise a box canyon *wadi* was chosen, and the German soldiers were told to imagine an SAS commando camping in it for the night. What they didn't know until the last minute was that Stirling and several of his men were actually there. "I withdrew the sentries," Stirling says ruefully, "to get them rested—stupid thing to do as it turned out. The Germans put in a model performance of capturing an SAS unit. There were a dozen or so of us and four to five hundred of them. We were really caught with our pants down."

He escaped again and did a reconnaissance of a German airfield, planning to return with two jeeps from his emergency base later and "have a go at it." But the plan went awry. "I went to sleep under a bush and forgot about the last foot or so of my anatomy. When I woke up there was a very large number of battalions around."

Perhaps the best testimonial to Stirling's military career came from Field Marshal Erwin Rommel himself. "With his capture," Rommel wrote, "the British lost the very able and adaptable commander of the desert group, which had caused us more damage than any other British unit of equal strength."

The blood of the Scottish border raiders that flows in David Stirling's veins and impelled him to high adventure in those far-off days still animates his personality today. He is still a romantic, an individualist, a crusader. His enemy today is no longer the Desert Fox but something much more amorphous—international communism. With his flawless manners and modest demeanor he encourages moderate British trade unionists to become more active in the movement, and Africans queue up in his outer office while, down below in the quiet courtyard, a tough-looking gentleman with a scarred face and cauliflower ears waits.

"It was nice to see you," he says, rising. "Do go and see G Squadron [SAS] in Hereford. It's changed a lot since my day. They're doing amazing things these days, amazing things."

241.

Appendices

Regimental Origins, Precedence and Rivalries

As with any geneaological subject rooted in the distant past, there is much debate, most of it good-humored, about the historical origins of the regiments that make up the Household Division. Confusion arises not only over the original date of a regiment's formation but also whether its service was continuous, the nature of its true allegiance, and when it became an official part of the sovereign's bodyguard.

The simplest explanation for the confusion is that the Guards—and indeed the British army as a whole—were forged in the heat of a civil war. Thus although the Coldstream Guards, whose motto is *Nulli Secundus* ("Second to None"), were formed six years before the Grenadiers and are the oldest continuously serving regiment in the British army, they are, nonetheless, second in line to the First or Grenadier Guards. That is because the Coldstream were raised under Cromwell while the Grenadiers were formed, and given immediate status as *Household* troops, by the exiled King Charles II. With the restoration of the monarchy, the Coldstream were made part of the royal bodyguard, and after the death of their founder, General George Monck, in 1670, they were officially designated what people had long called them, the Coldstream Guards.

The Scots Guards were formed before either the Coldstream or the Grenadiers. But they had the misfortune to be on the losing side during the Civil War—unlike the wily Monck and his men from the

Scottish border—and were disbanded by Cromwell. By the time they had been re-formed and given royal bodyguard status, they had to go to the end of the line and were designated the Third Regiment of Foot Guards. Queen Victoria restored their ethnic title in 1877 when they once again became the Scots Guards.

The Irish Guards were formed in 1900 but trace their beginnings back to the seventeenth century, around the time of the Civil War, and through the Irish Brigade that fought for the French with distinction in the eighteenth century. Known as the "Wild Geese," they broke the British Guards' line in the Battle of Fontenoy, capturing colors, cannon and prisoners. The Welsh Guards, the youngest of the Foot Guards family and the least controversial, were created in the middle of the 1914–18 War.

Turning to the Household Cavalry, the Life Guards are the senior though not the oldest regiment in the army. They are always positioned on the right of the line on parade unless the King's Troop, Royal Horse Artillery, is present with its guns. The Royal Horse Guards (the Blues) trace their origins to a regiment raised under Cromwell in the New Model Army that, after the return of King Charles II, was renamed the Royal Regiment of Horse and put under the command of the Earl of Oxford, whose blue livery gave the regiment its nickname. In 1687 it was renamed again, the Royal Horse Guards, but it was not granted full status as Household regiment until 1820, in recognition of its conduct at Waterloo and as a compliment to the Duke of Wellington, the regiment's colonel.

The Royal Dragoon Guards, the oldest line cavalry regiment in the army, began its career with twenty-two years of fighting the Moors in Morocco defending Tangier for Charles II. Three hundred years later, in 1969, the regiment was amalgamated with the Royal Horse Guards to become the Blues and Royals.

The loyalties of the Guards regiments were often stretched by the changing fortunes of England's kings. The Coldstream and the Blues fought under Cromwell against the Royalists, while Scots and Irish fought for the Catholic Stuarts against the Protestant Hanoverians. Occasionally, a ritualistic detail that provides an echo of those uncertain times survives. The Scots Guards, for example, used to pass their glasses over their finger bowls when drinking the loyal toast, indicating that they were paying homage to the exiled Jacobite pretender—"the king across the water"—rather than to the Hanoverian incumbent. The practice came to the notice of the authorities, and finger bowls were banned forever in Scots Guards' messes.

Trooping the Color

The origins of the ritual are older than the British army itself. In medieval warfare each military leader had a color, or standard, around which his men would rally on the march or in battle. The problem was ensuring that everyone knew what it looked like, so it became customary at the end of the day to carry the colors along the ranks and escort them back to the billet or wherever they were to be kept for the night.

There was another reason for the ceremony. When a unit was in a strange place, it was important for everyone to know where to muster in the event of an emergency. The colors were therefore hung from a doorway or window to mark the company's headquarters. Each morning they were solemnly taken back to their place in the ranks. As time went on the colors became the symbol of a unit, and today they are accorded respect approaching veneration, rather in the manner that altar vessels and vestments are treated by the clergy.

It became traditional for young officers—ensigns in the Foot Guards and cornets in the cavalry—to carry the colors on parade and into battle, and they were protected by "color" sergeants, a rank that still survives. The last time the Guards took their colors onto the battlefield was at Inkerman in the Crimea in 1854, a bloody maul fought in swirling fog.

Colors are "laid up" after a decade or so and spend the remainder of eternity in hallowed precincts associated with the regiment, usually a church, school or museum. Apart from the regimental and Queen's colors, there are personal standards for officers within a regiment: the commanding officer's color, the adjutant's color and so on. These can be kept by the title holder after he leaves his job, but they must be paid for; they are costly items made of hand-embroidered silk.

In the old days there was a less reverential use for the colors. There used to be a tradition that newly joined ensigns would have to prove their virility with one of London's ladies of easy virtue in front of their brother officers in the mess. The scene of the action was the dining-room table with the regimental color draped over it.

Detail of helmet, Life Guards (opposite page)

Historical Chronology

1642
Scots Guards raised by King Charles I and sent to Ireland to suppress a rebellion.

1642–49
English Civil Wars (Royalists versus Roundheads). Ascendancy of Oliver Cromwell and his parliamentary forces. Execution of King Charles I in Whitehall, January 30, 1649.

1650
Colonel George Monck's regiment of foot raised in the small Scottish border town of Coldstream as part of Cromwell's New Model Army—Britain's first regular military force; it later became the Coldstream Guards. In the same year, a cavalry regiment was raised and commanded by James Berry under Cromwell; this unit later became the Royal Horse Guards (the Blues).

1651
Scots Guards disbanded by Cromwell after the defeat of the King's son (the future Charles II) at the Battle of Worcester. Charles fled to the Continent.

1656
While in exile, Charles raised a "Royal Regiment of Guards" from among his followers and gave them the status of "Household" troops. This unit later became the First or Grenadier Regiment of Foot Guards.

1659
A similar protective unit of cavalry was formed by Charles and called the Horse Guards or Life Guard of Horse—the origin of the Life Guards.

1660
Monck marched to London with his "Coldstreamers" to help Parliament restore the monarchy, Cromwell having died two years earlier. Return of Charles II from exile. Scots Guards re-formed but this time as part of the Scottish army. They were later incorporated into the English forces as the Third Regiment of Foot Guards—after the First (Grenadier) and the Second (Coldstream) Guards—but eventually regained their original title of Scots Guards.

1661
A cavalry regiment known as the "Tangier Horse" was formed to defend the town of Tangier in Morocco, a newly acquired possession of the Crown. This regiment later became the Royal Dragoon Guards and much later still amalgamated with the Royal Horse Guards (the Blues) to form the Blues and Royals.

1662
The Household Division (apart from the Irish and Welsh Guards, which were created in the early twentieth century) was established in fact if not in name with soldiers who had fought against each other in the Civil War and were now reunited under the restored monarchy.

1664
The Coldstream Guards provided a detachment to capture New Amsterdam, capital of the Dutch settlements in North America. The commander of the expedition, who, curiously, held a captain's rank in both the Coldstream and the Royal Navy, renamed the colony New York in honor of Charles II's brother, the Duke of York. (The first military actions of the Guards frequently involved fighting at sea. General Monck himself commanded ships in several sea battles, with mixed results and probably not helped by his habit of ordering his fleet to "wheel" and "charge.")

1674

Following a threat on his life, Charles II gave the special task of protecting himself and his queen to the Life Guards, who had been guarding the royal family within the palace for a decade. The King's new decree enjoined the Life Guards to "attend the King's person on foot wheresoever he walk, from his rising to his going to bed and this is performed by one of the three Captains, who always waits immediately next to the King's own person before all others carrying in his hand an ebony staff or truncheon with a gold head, engraved with His Majesty's cypher and crown. . . . Near him also attends another principal Commissioned Officer with an ebony staff and silver head, who is ready to relieve the Captain on occassions."

The royal appointments, Gold and Silver Sticks-in-Waiting, which often baffle people today, date from the real need to protect the royal family in more turbulent times. Gold Stick-in-Waiting is held nowadays by the colonels of the Household Cavalry regiments, in turn, a month at a time each. The Silver Stick post is held by one of the commanding officers of the Household Cavalry.

1680

First battle honors (Tangier) awarded to the First (Grenadier) Guards, the Coldstream and the Royal Horse Guards (the Blues).

1693

Life Guards saved King William III from capture at the battle of Landen.

1702–13

War of Spanish Succession. Notable for the Duke of Marlborough's (formerly John Churchill of the Grenadier Guards) spectacular victories over the French. However, while the Guards were popular abroad, they were anything but heroes at home. Appalling pay, a rough criminal leavening, and savage punishment resulted in an unruly and unreliable military presence in London where the Guards were often used as policemen. A common duty was the provision of escorts for criminals being taken from prisons in the City of London up to "Tyburn Tree" (modern-day Marble Arch) and hanged in front of the drunken, jeering mob.

1740–48

War of Austrian Succession. Another confused and protracted dynastic struggle, in which the Life Guards, the Blues, the Royal Dragoon Guards, and all three regiments of Foot Guards took part.

Battle of Dettingen (June 27, 1743).

Interesting as the last battle in which a king of England fought at the head of his troops. Escorted by Gold Stick and a faithful detachment of Life Guards, George II promptly led his men into a trap. Nevertheless, he fought bravely, and despite his horse bolting managed to muddle through, turning a potential rout into a victory. The victory would have been more conclusive if the king had pursued the defeated French, but he declined that opportunity and instead retired to the shade of an oak tree, where he demolished a large lunch of cold mutton.

Battle of Fontenoy (May 11, 1745).

George II turned over command to his twenty-five-year-old son, the Duke of Cumberland, and the battle ended in a bloody defeat. But there were some highlights for the Guards, who were pitted against the French Guards regiments for the first time. At one climactic stage in the battle the British and French Guards found themselves some thirty yards apart. Lord Charles Hay, then a captain in the Grenadiers, stepped forward, doffed his hat, pulled out a flask, and drank a toast to the astonished French. The French version of the incident, ascribed to Voltaire, has Lord Hay saying: "Gentlemen of the French Guards, fire first." To which the French commander allegedly replied: "No, sir, we never fire first," but promptly unleashed a volley, which, fortunately for the British, went high. The Guards responded with a model demonstration of fire and movement and advanced triumphantly through the decimated ranks of their opponents. However, their Dutch allies failed to support them and the French threw in more troops, including the Irish Brigade, which had been fighting as highly valued mercenaries for the French ever since the defeat of the Roman Catholic James II at the Battle of the Boyne in 1690. The day ended in a disastrous defeat for the British and their allies, with each of the Guards battalions losing roughly half their men. Two footnotes to the battle: the Irish Brigade captured two of the Coldstream Guards colors, and Lord Hay was seriously wounded. He recovered, but was later court-martialed for making insubordinate remarks about his Commander-in-Chief in Canada—he accused his superior of "making sham sieges and planting cabbages when he ought to have been fighting." He died while awaiting sentence.

1745–46

The Jacobite Rebellion. Defeat of Bonnie Prince Charlie's attempt to restore the Stuarts to the throne. The Guards took part in the defense of London and the pursuit of the Jacobite forces to Scotland, but not in the final bloody denouement on Culloden Moor in 1746.

1756–63 The Seven Years War.

Battle of Warburg (July 31, 1760).
The British cavalry was led by John Manners, Marquess of Granby, Colonel of the Royal Horse Guards (the Blues). During the action both his hat and wig blew off. His squadrons followed his gleaming bald head in a breathless and totally successful pursuit of the enemy, and as the victory passed into the annals of British military history, the phrase "going baldheaded for it" made its way into the English language. Lord Granby still in his naked state, later saluted the army commander, and ever since the Blues have retained the custom of saluting their officers even when hatless— the only unit in the British army permitted to do so. Granby returned to England a hero. He was also popular with his men and set many of them up as publicans after they left the army, an act of generosity that accounts for the inordinate number of pubs in Britain today called the "Marquess of Granby."

1776–83

The Guards in America. For the second time in their history, the Guards captured New York. This time the First (Grenadier) and the Third (Scots) Guards were involved, and their enemies were the American colonists. When the Guards left England King George III gave permission for the officers "to make up an uniform with white lace and the sergeants to have their coats laced with white instead of gold." The King would have done better to have them exchange their bright scarlet tunics for leather jackets and coonskins in order to combat the new and devastating guerrilla tactics of the colonists. The Guards fought bravely enough during the war, but the final surrender by Lord Cornwallis at Yorktown (October 19, 1781), with six thousand men, five hundred of whom were Guardsmen, was one of their least glorious military actions. Casualties usually tell a tale, and on that occasion the Guards only lost a major, a sergeant, and three Guardsmen.

1793

Start of the French Revolutionary and Napoleonic Wars. Officers Mess built in St. James's Palace for officers of the guard doing duty there and at Horse Guards. Army regulations provided for a nightly dinner for thirteen officers, consisting of "two regular courses and a dessert with port, sherry, madeira, wines, ale, porter, and table beer."

1793–95

British Expeditionary Force fought the French revolutionary armies in the Low Countries. The Foot Guards and the Blues took part in these inconclusive battles before returning home.

1801

In a seaborne assault on Aboukir Bay, a British force, which included a Guards brigade, defeated the French army that Napoleon had left behind in Egypt. The

Drum Major and members of the Corps of Drums, 2nd Battalion Scots Guards (opposite page)

Coldstream and Scots Guards still bear a badge of the Sphinx on their colors, recalling their part in that campaign.

1803–04

Guards deployed to defend London against Napoleon's threat to invade England, in much the same way as they were to be used almost 150 years later when Hitler threatened invasion.

1808–14

The Peninsular War. Dispatch of a British force under thirty-nine-year-old Sir Arthur Wellesley (later the Duke of Wellington) to Portugal. A second force under Sir John Moore went to northwestern Spain. The Peninsular campaign began, as did so many in Britain's military history, with a retreat. On December 26, 1808, Moore's army, outnumbered by the French two to one, started a three-week rear-guard action to its lifeline to the Royal Navy at the port of Corunna. Sir John Fortescue, in his *History of the British Army*, re-creates the scene as General Moore watched his exhausted and bedraggled troops stumble into Corunna—a scene that has become famous in Guards lore:

"A brigade caught the General's eye at a distance, for they were marching like soldiers.

"'Those must be the Guards,' he said, and presently the two battalions of the First Guards, each of them still eight hundred strong, strode by in column of sections, with drums beating, the drum major twirling his staff at their head and the men keeping step as if in their own barrack yard. . . ."

All the Household regiments fought with Wellington in the protracted Peninsular campaign, which lasted five years and ended victoriously with the expulsion of the French from the Iberian peninsula and the abdication of Napoleon. Although the Guards had not taken part in any particularly oustanding actions, they had impressed their commander, who declared they had set "a laudable example" to the rest of the army. Wellington, however, was less amused by the Grenadier Guards officers' practice of sitting under umbrellas during a bombardment, and he sent them a stern message saying that he would not allow "gentlemen's sons to make themselves ridiculous in the eyes of the Army."

1815

End of the Napoleonic Wars at the *Battle of Waterloo* (June 18, 1815).
Seen through a military historian's lens, the Peninsular War can perhaps be thought of as an arduous but necessary prelude to the British army's finest hour and one of the most glorious episodes in Guards' long and distinguished record. For the victory at Waterloo not only crushed Napoleon and ended twenty years of warfare but opened an era of unprecedented peace and prosperity in Europe. "The worst army I ever commanded," was Wellington's acerbic comment at the beginning of the short campaign that led to the battle. He later admitted that he had been unnecessarily pessimistic. The Guards were represented in the battle by a brigade of Household Cavalry and two brigades of Foot Guards. The battle had a number of dramatic moments, but three stand out in the Guards' history. The first was the defense of the Château Hougoumont, a position crucial to Wellington's strategy, which was held desperately but successfully by the Coldstream and the Third (Scots) Guards. Wellington later said that the success of the battle turned upon the closing of the gates of Hougoumont by the Coldstream Guards. The second event was the routing of the 105th French infantry regiment by the Royal Dragoon Guards. The cavalrymen captured the enemy's standard with its imperial eagle, and the bird is still featured today on the Blues and Royals' uniform. The third incident was perhaps the most spectacular of all. As a last throw, Napoleon ordered his carefully husbanded Grenadiers of the Imperial Guard—soldiers who had marched and fought on every battlefield in Europe and had never been defeated—against the British infantry. The First Guards took the brunt of the attack, checked it, and hurled the French back in disorder. The action broke the back of Napoleon's army and decided the day. To commemorate their triumph, the First Guards were named "Grenadier"

Guards—the grenade is still worn as a cap and collar badge—and the Imperial Guards' tall bearskin caps became their official headdress. (It was not until 1832 that the Coldstream and Scots Guards also adopted the bearskin.)

No story of Waterloo, no matter how brief, is complete without the "Uxbridge incident." Lord Uxbridge, commander of the heavy cavalry and later Colonel of the Blues, was struck by a cannonball in the dying moments of the battle as he sat on his horse beside Wellington.

"By God, sir," his Lordship is alleged to have cried, "I've lost a leg!"

Wellington looked down. "By God, sir," he said, "so you have."

Uxbridge's leg—he lived to the ripe old age of eight-five—was buried at Waterloo, and the artificial limb he had made on his return to England is now in the Household Cavalry museum in Windsor, along with the plaster cast of the skull of Corporal Shaw of the Life Guards, a famous pugilist, who did mighty work during the battle before being killed.

1816–54

Peace in Europe, prosperity at home, stagnation in the army. As in previous—and future—times of international calm, the Guards were fully occupied at home as London's policemen, strikebreakers, riot suppressors (one such suppression earned the Life Guards the tag of the "Butchers of Piccadilly"), and ceremonial troops.

1854–56

The Crimean War. Notable for the British and French fighting together rather than against each other, though it did not stop the British commander-in-chief, who was a Waterloo veteran, from repeatedly referring to the enemy (Russians to a man) as the "French." The Guards were in the thick of the fighting, carrying their colors into battle for the last time, and won thirteen of a newly struck medal for valor, the Victoria Cross. The war was also notable for the innovation of military nursing under Florence Nightingale and for front-line newspaper reporting pioneered by William Russell of the London *Times*.

1871

Edward Cardwell's army reforms abolished flogging and the purchase and sale of commissions, both hallowed army institutions.

1882

The Household Cavalry was dispatched to Egypt to quell an anti-European insurgency. In a moonlit charge across the desert, the cavalry defeated the rebels.

1884

Sudan. General Gordon was sent to evacuate the garrison at Khartoum, which was under pressure from the Mahdi and his fanatical Muslim followers. Gordon, a romantic and eccentric, spent his last night with the Blues in their London barracks. However, since he was not suitably attired for dinner, he had to sit in the anteroom of the officers' mess and eat his supper off a tray. Gordon and his small force were quickly besieged in Khartoum and a relief force, which included a Heavy Camel Regiment drawn from the Household Cavalry, arrived too late. The British garrison was overrun and Gordon killed. An even more practical innovation than camels accompanied this campaign. The Guards were, for the first time, allowed to wear khaki uniforms—as the Indian army had done for some time—to the distress of Queen Victoria, who did not like the "café au lait" shade at all.

1899–1902

The Boer War. This bitter struggle against the fast-moving Afrikaner farmers on the South African veldt took the British by surprise, rather in the manner that the guerrilla tactics of the American colonists had upset military thinking more than a century earlier. The Foot Guards, not for the first time, became cavalrymen to combat the elusive Boer sharpshooters, who, apart from giving the British a hard time, donated the word "commando" to the English language.

*From left
to right,
top to
bottom:*

*Officer,
Blues & Royals*

*Officer,
Irish Guards,
in Mess Kit*

*Pipe Major,
Scots Guards*

*Officer,
Scots Guards,
in Frock Coat
Order*

*Musician,
Scots Guards*

*Piper,
Irish Guards*

*Drummer,
Scots Guards*

*NCO,
Coldstream
Guards*

*Officer,
Life Guards*

*Grenadier
Guardsman
in Greatcoat
Order*

*NCO,
Irish Guards,
in No. 1 Dress*

*Musician,
Irish Guards*

*Piper,
Irish Guards*

*Officer,
Irish Guards,
in Service
Dress*

*NCO,
Coldstream
Guards*

*Musician,
Grenadier
Guards*

From left to right, top to bottom:

Warrant Officer, Scots Guards, in No. 2 Dress

Drum Major Scots Guards, in State Dress with Cloak

Officer, Scots Guards, in Service Dress

Officer, Life Guards, in Dismounted Review Order

Lance Corporal, Irish Guards

NCO, Scots Guards, in Winter Guard Order

Bass Drummer, Scots Guards

Officer, Welsh Guards

Officer, Coldstream Guards, in Winter Guard Order

Officer, Coldstream Guards, in No. 1 Dress

Drum Major, Scots Guards, in Guard Order

Director of Music, Welsh Guards

Regimental Sergeant Major, Scots Guards

Officer, Grenadier Guards, in Service Dress

NCO, Blues & Royals

Officer, Scots Guards

Formation of the Irish Guards (April 1). The royal citation read: "Her Majesty the Queen, having deemed it desirable to commemorate the bravery shown by the Irish Regiments during the operations in South Africa in the years 1899–1900 has been graciously pleased that an Irish Regiment of Foot Guards be formed and designated the 'Irish Guards.'"

1905–12

Lord Haldane, Secretary of State for War, introduced a series of reforms that transformed the army from a museum piece into a modern and highly professional force—which was fortunate, since war broke out two years later.

1914

Start of First World War. A war that began with vast public enthusiasm and expectation of a rapid victory; that had the Household Cavalry on horses, on their feet, on bicycles, as artillerymen, and finally as machine-gunners; a war that yet again began with a retreat (Mons) where the Foot Guards set the style, as they had done at Corunna in the Peninsular War; a conflict that virtually wiped out Britain's best professional army since Cromwell's day; a war, by all appearances, that would go on forever in the glutinous Flanders mud.

1915

Formation of the Welsh Guards (March 1). The bulk of the new regiment was made up of Welshmen serving in the Grenadier Guards, and on St. David's Day—the day honoring Wales's patron saint—the new unit mounted the King's Guard at Buckingham Palace. Creation of the Guards Division.

1918

First World War, the "war to end all wars" finally came to an end in November, destroying millions of lives and resolving nothing.

1919–39

The brief peace. Ceremonial largely replaced active soldiering but there were also some peacekeeping duties at home, during the postwar unrest and the General Strike of 1926, and abroad, in troublesome colonies such as Palestine. A time of military cuts. In the 1920's the First and Second Life Guards were amalgamated and a threat to disband the Irish and Welsh Guards was narrowly averted. There was also much inconclusive debate on rearmament to meet the growing German threat.

1939–45

Second World War. Palace guards continued during the war, but in khaki battle dress and steel helmets. The cavalry arrived at Horse Guards in a furniture van or an old bus, but the Foot Guards marched as usual despite German bombs and rockets. The aerial attack on London resulted in one tragedy for the Guards. During Sunday morning services on June 18, 1944, a flying bomb scored a direct hit on the Guards Chapel in Wellington Barracks, within drill instructor's call of Buckingham Palace, and killed 121 people inside. The entire building was destroyed except for the apse; the cross over the altar remained upright and the candles continued burning. At home, the Guards, reverting to their historical role of sovereign's bodyguard, provided special escorts for the King, the royal family, and the Prime Minister. They also guarded Rudolph Hess, the German leader who parachuted into Britain to try to make peace, in the Tower of London and are, ironically, still guarding him today in Berlin's Spandau prison.

The Guards were involved in every major theater of war except the Far East—Norway, Dunkirk (another retreat, where 330,000 men of the British Expeditionary Force, including six battalions of Foot Guards, returned safely to England), North Africa, Italy, Normandy, Arnhem and the crossing of the Rhine.

Desert War. The Guards fought throughout the North African campaign and in doing so played a significant part in creating three highly innovative military organizations. These were the No. 8 Commando unit, the Long Range Desert Group, and the Special Air Service, all of which were launched and commanded by Guards officers: Brigadier Robert Laycock (the Blues), Major Michael Crichton-Stuart (Scots Guards), and Lieutenant David Stirling (Scots Guards) respectively.

Italy. Probably the single most traumatic campaign of the war for the Guards. The battle at Anzio resulted in the virtual annihilation of the First Battalion of the Irish Guards, and three other Guards battalions lost about eighty percent of their men.

The Guards Armored Division. Formed in May, 1941, for the invasion of the European continent, which took place three years later. It was an original concept—turning some of the best infantry in the world into armored cavalrymen—but it worked. The division adopted the insignia of the "ever-open eye," which had been the emblem of the Guards Division in the First World War. The Armored Division's most famous exploit was the hundred-mile dash in a day to liberate Brussels, a race between the Grenadiers and the Welsh Guards, which the latter narrowly won. The Division's least glorious moment was the misconceived Arnhem airborne operation, where it had the virtually impossible task of fighting along a single heavily defended road to link up with the beleaguered airborne troops in Arnhem. The Guards' tanks managed to reach Nijmegen and secure the town's important road bridge across the Waal, but the Germans denied them their ultimate objective, the "bridge too far" in General Frederick "Boy" Browning's telling phrase.

1946–67

End of Empire. The Guards reverted to their familiar postwar duties: guard mounting in tunic and bearskin, taking over public utilities during strikes, and policing rebellious colonies. A new phenomenon emerged in 1947 and lasted until 1962: peacetime conscription, which involved two years of "national service" in the armed forces for all Britain's young men. As the empire was unraveled and discarded, the Guards "kept the peace" in places as far-flung as Palestine, Malaya, Hong Kong, Kenya, the Cameroons, British Guiana, Cyprus, Borneo, and Aden.

1968

A reorganization did away with the familiar "Brigade of Guards" (all Foot Guards) and produced a composite and much tidier entity called the Household Division, which brought the Foot Guards and the Household Cavalry closer together in a single administrative unit.

1969

A sharp budgetary axe wielded by the government trimmed the army severely, disbanding many famous regiments and amalgamating others. The Guards' worst casualty was the amalgamation of the Royal Horse Guards (the Blues) with the senior line cavalry regiment, the Royal Dragoon Guards, to produce the Blues and Royals.

A different kind of shock came with the disturbances in Northern Ireland. All the Guards regiments except the Irish Guards have spent regular tours of duty there—the cavalry acting as infantry—and have suffered many casualties in the mean streets of Belfast and the deceptively peaceful Irish countryside.

1973

End of the Bank of England "picquet," a ceremonial responsibility of the Guards dating back to the Gordon Riots in 1780. The Tower of London Guard, with its seven-hundred-year-old "ceremony of the keys," continues, as do the Horse Guards and royal palaces guard mountings.

1978

Queen Elizabeth II's Silver Jubilee.

Detail of back of tunic of the Blues and Royals (page 256)